GrowerTalks® *on*
Perennials

Edited by

Rick Blanchette

Ball Publishing
Batavia, Illinois, U.S.A.

Ball Publishing
Post Office Box 9
335 North River Street
Batavia, IL 60510, USA
www.ballpublishing.com

Cover design by Christine Victor, Batavia, Illinois.
Interior design by Bay Graphics, Williams Bay, Wisconsin.

Library of Congress Cataloging-in-Publication Data

GrowerTalks on perennials / edited by Rick Blanchette.
   p. cm.
  ISBN 1-883052-32-7 (alk. paper)
  1. Perennials. I. Blanchette, Rick, 1966-
  SB434 .G76 2002
  635.9'32—dc21

              2002005753

Printed in the United States of America
07 06 05 04 03 02 1 2 3 4 5 6

Contents

Chapter 7: Grower Profiles

Contributing Authors

Allen Armitage is professor, horticulture department, University of Georgia, Athens.

Chris Beytes is editor of *GrowerTalks* magazine.

Tim Brindley is vice president of operations, Stacy's Greenhouses, York, South Carolina.

Arthur C. Cameron is professor of horticulture, Department of Horticulture, Michigan State University, East Lansing, Michigan.

William H. Carlson is professor of horticulture, Department of Horticulture, Michigan State University, East Lansing, Michigan.

Stephanie Cohen is director of the Mid-Atlantic Region of the Perennial Plant Association and adjunct professor and director of the landscape arboretum, Temple University, Ambler, Pennsylvania.

Danziger Dan Flower Farm, Beit Dagan, Israel

Gary Doerr, Peppergrove Nurseries, Lapeer, Michigan.

Roger Elliot, Koala Blooms, Victoria, Australia.

Beth Engle is a former graduate student at Michigan State University, East Lansing.

John Friel is marketing manager of Yoder Brothers' Green Leaf Perennials brand and a freelance writer.

Cheryl K. Hamaker is a former a graduate student at Michigan State University, East Lansing.

Harlan Hamernik is owner of Bluebird Nursery Inc., Clarkson, Nebraska.

Debbie Hamrick is editor of *FloraCulture International* magazine and contributing editor for *GrowerTalks* magazine.

Mary Harris is a research associate, Entomology Department, University of Georgia Experiment Station, Griffin, Georgia.

Royal D. Heins is professor of horticulture, Department of Horticulture, Michigan State University, East Lansing.

Paul Koreman is a graduate student, Michigan State University, East Lansing.

Joanne Lutz is an IPM scouting specialist based in Wheaton, Maryland, with her own business, Joanne's IPM Inc.

Jeff McGrew is director, North America, for Kieft Bloemzaden B.V., Venhuizen, the Netherlands. He is based in Mount Vernon, Washington.

Jim Nau is trials and varieties manager, Ball Horticultural Co., West Chicago, Illinois, and author of the *Ball Perennial Manual* and *Ball Culture Guide.*

Joseph C. Neal is professor of weed science, Department of Horticultural Science, North Carolina State University, Raleigh.

Kerstin Ouellet is president of Pen & Petal, Fallbrook, California.

Paul Pilon is head grower, Sawyer Nursery, Hudsonville, Michigan.

Martha Simon Pindale is president, Bluemount Nurseries Inc., Monkton, Maryland.

Conrad Richter is vice president of Richters Herbs, Goodwood, Ontario, Canada.

Erik S. Runkle is a former graduate student at Michigan State University, East Lansing.

Cathy St. Pierre is a marketing consultant specializing in the horticultural industry, based in Lawrence, Massachusetts.

Cheryl Smith is a plant health extension specialist, University of New Hampshire Cooperative Extension, Durham.

Steven Still is executive director of the Perennial Plant Association, Hilliard, Ohio.

Ellen Talmage is director of marketing, Talmage Farm, Riverhead, New York.

Rob Wein, Clearview Horticultural Products, Aldergrove, British Columbia, Canada.

Cathy Whitman is a freelance writer from Holt, Michigan.

Paul and **Paula Yantorno** are part owners of Center Greenhouses, Denver, Colorado.

Mei Yuan is a former graduate student at Michigan State University, East Lansing.

Introduction

Perennials are booming. As a result, many growers are trying their hand at this category. Traditional bedding plant growers and nurserymen have both joined the fray, competing along with those growers who have always specialized in perennials.

One of the most challenging part of growing perennials is that there has been little information about each crop, and what is true for one crop may be completely opposite for the next. Growers have thus been forced to experiment with each plant with few guidelines. But as the segment has grown, so has the amount of research being done on scheduling, forcing, and using growth regulators. Royal Heins at Michigan State and Allan Armitage at Georgia have led the way and are but a few of the academics contributing to the cause. And as growers have success, they are sharing their knowledge of what works and what doesn't with others so the industry as a whole can improve and grow.

As this information has become available, *GrowerTalks* magazine has been sharing it with you. The material found in *GrowerTalks on Perennials* is a sampling of articles that have appeared over the past several years. You'll find research on the still controversial issue of forcing perennials to flower out of season. The use of plant growth regulators has received a lot of attention recently, and you'll find the latest information right here. In fact, we've included a chart listing PGRs and their effectiveness on over 150 different perennials!

Other topics covered in *GrowerTalks on Perennials* are propagation, pest and disease control, and crop culture for a variety of important species. We have also included a chapter on marketing, featuring articles from the Perennial Cynic, John Friel. And the book would not be complete without grower profiles, highlighting those growers who have caught our attention through innovation, diligence, or quality.

As always, we recommend that you trial before trying anything you read in this volume. What has worked for growers and researchers may not be best for your situation, and it's best to try new methods on a small sampling of plants so you do not jeopardize an entire crop.

Chapter 1
Crops and Culture

Fabulous Fountain Grass
Kerstin P. Ouellet

Ornamental grasses are quickly gaining popularity among home gardeners. They're favorites for the landscape, where they create stunning effects with little care and maintenance. An alternative application for ornamental grasses is their use in container gardens. From the stately 4 ft. of purple fountain grass in the center of a large container to the delicate 3 to 4 in. tall Carmel carpet sedge (*Carex bergrenii*), even the most discriminating container gardener is bound to find a variety that meets their need.

One of the most popular species of ornamental grasses is *Pennisetum*, or fountain grass. *Pennisetum* is a genus with over a hundred different species, native to both tropical and temperate regions. Their hardiness ranges from Zone 5 to Zone 10, depending on the species. In areas where they're not frost hardy, they can effectively be grown as annuals.

The showy flowers of *Pennisetum* can be up to 12 in. long and range in color from white over cream, pink, red, and brown to almost black, resembling a foxtail shape. They're also excellent as cut flowers.

Probably the best-selling species is *Pennisetum setaceum*, or tender fountain grass. The following cultural recommendations refer to *P. setaceum* in particular, although some of the information is applicable to other species as well.

Propagation. Although *Pennisetum* can easily be grown from seed—

Whether in a container or in the landscape, the popular, easy-to-grow fountain grasses (*Pennisetum*) are sure winners.

1

some species have even naturalized freely in mild climates—the recommended method is to start from liners propagated by division, which saves a lot of time in propagation. Some of the most popular cultivars can't successfully be grown from seed because they either don't produce viable seed or the seedlings aren't true to type.

Media. *Pennisetum* adapts to many different types of soils, but performs best in moist, well-drained, fertile growing medium. Avoid boggy soils, as they'll cause floppy growth. Keep growing medium evenly moist, but avoid overwatering.

Fertilizer. Ornamental grasses require minimal fertilizer. Choose a fertilizer high in nitrogen and apply a constant feed of 50 ppm or a periodic feed with 100 ppm.

Light. *Pennisetum* performs best in full sun, but can tolerate light shade. Too much shade will make the plants flop. Northern growers may want to use supplemental lighting for spring crops. This speeds growth significantly.

Temperature. *Pennisetum setaceum* is a warm-season grass. It's grown as an annual in regions colder than Zone 9. Ideal growing temperatures for a quick greenhouse crop are 70 to 85°F during the day and 70°F at night. Lower temperatures are possible, but will lengthen the crop time. *Pennisetum* can be grown outdoors once the nights are frost-free.

There's very little data available for growing ornamental grasses in greenhouse conditions. You should experiment to find the conditions that are ideal for your circumstances.

Pests. There are no known insect or disease problems that affect *Pennisetum* as long as good sanitation practices are followed.

Varieties. *P. setaceum* 'Rubrum' may very well be the best-selling ornamental grass in North America. 'Rubrum' has deep burgundy-colored foliage and purple foxtail flowers that turn cream as they mature. It forms clumps up to 4 ft. tall and is superb as a specimen in large container gardens or in the landscape.

P. setaceum 'Red Riding Hood' could be called the best fountain grass for container gardens. Its foliage and flowers are just as beautiful as those of 'Rubrum', but it's much better behaved, with a mature height of only 18 to 30 in.

P. messiacum 'Red Bunny Tails' has glossy green foliage with burgundy highlights. Its soft, stocky flower plumes are dark burgundy red and super-soft to the touch. With a mature height of only 16 to 18 in., 'Red Bunny Tails' is versatile in container gardens and the landscape. It can withstand slightly colder temperatures and is frost hardy to Zone 8.

October 2001

Bread-and-Butter Perennials

Chris Beytes and Martha Simon Pindale

Are your bedding plant sales going stale? These fifteen bread-and-butter varieties are the perfect introduction to perennials for growers, retailers, and landscapers.

With literally thousands of perennial species to choose from, deciding which ones your business should carry can be a daunting task. Do you specialize in hostas and stock a hundred different varieties? Do you force perennials for mass market spring sales? Or do you try to be a one-stop shop by carrying a little bit of everything? Tough decisions, indeed.

If you're not sure what end of the perennial business you want to target but want a safe starting place, we can help. We've picked out—with the help of Bluemount Nurseries' Martha Simon Pindale and *Ball Perennial Manual* author Jim Nau—fifteen bread-and-butter perennials that every grower, retailer, and landscaper should try.

Martha has provided her comments about each variety, along with tips and tricks she's gleaned from a lifetime in the perennial business. They're all easy to grow, relatively carefree, provide great color and plant habit, and offer a variety of bloom times and plant habits for both sun and shade. Photos, except where noted, are courtesy of Bluemount Nurseries.

Helianthemum (Rock Rose)

Who says there are no evergreen perennials? Technically subshrubs, *Helianthemum* are not only ever-green, they're tough and low maintenance. Their low growing habit makes them perfect for edging or for tumbling over retaining walls.

They're available in a myriad of colors—try the gray foliaged varieties such as 'Wisley Pink' (pink flowers with yellow centers) or 'Henfield Brilliant' (bright orange flowers) or the green foliaged 'Cerise Queen' (double red blooms) or 'Buttercup' (yellow flowers). And that's just for starters! Rock roses need excellent drainage and thrive in hot, sunny locations. Propagate by tip cuttings.

Artemisia

This stunning foliage plant has finely cut silver leaves that pair up wonderfully with other plants. Its ability to thrive in hot, dry sites and in poor soil makes this tough plant a good choice for commercial sites. A fast grower that reaches 36 in. by 36 in., it has woody stems that can be cut back hard each spring, like *Buddleia*. Hardy to Zone 6, it's very heat tolerant and pest free. This *Artemisia* looks beautiful all summer long! Propagate by tip cuttings.

Convallaria majalis (Lily of the Valley)

Landscaping in shady areas is a challenge, but not if you plant *Convallaria*. An outstanding groundcover that's easy to grow and quick to spread, *Convallaria* with its lace-shaped leaves looks good all summer long. Deliciously fragrant white bells emerge with the leaves in early spring. Hot weather is its downfall, so Southern gardeners should pass on this plant. *Convallaria* grows best in Zones 2 to 6. Propagate by division.

Echinacea 'Magnus' (Purple Coneflower)

A magnificent native plant is finally becoming a landscape stable! Tough as nails and showy to boot, the midsummer blooms have large brown central cones ringed by rose-purple petals. The petals of the straight species hang down, but 'Magnus' is known for its flatter, more rose-colored petals. Magnus thrives in full sun to part shade and is grown from seed. An excellent cut flower, this beauty attracts wildlife. Butterflies visit the flowers all summer, and gold finches dive bomb the seed heads in the fall. 'Magnus' is the Perennial Plant Association's 1998 plant of the year. *Photo by Ball Publishing.*

Hemerocallis 'Stella d'Oro' (Daylily)

Landscapers have known for years that daylilies are excellent, carefree performers. So when the repeat blooming 'Stella d'Oro' came along, it created a lot of excitement. True, the rich orange flowers aren't as big as some other hybrids, and the plant does take a rest after the first flush of July flowers. But if the old flower stalks are removed, 'Stella d'Oro' will reward your efforts with flowers until frost. Full sun to part shade is where it grows best. It's hardy in Zones 4 to 9 and looks great in mass plantings.

Hosta

The workhorses of the shade garden, hostas come in thousands of different leaf colors, leaf shapes, and heights. Did I mention that they also have lavender or white flowers? Long-lived and durable, they're hardy in Zones 3 to 7. The leaves are fast growing and are good for hiding the foliage of spring bulbs. It's hard to pick the best hostas because there are so many available! For large specimens try 'Frances Williams' (above, left) with its blue-green leaves and golden margins or maybe the taller, vase-shaped 'Krossa Regal' (above, center). A medium-sized grower, 'Francee' (above, right) has deep green leaves and crisp white edges, while smaller types like 'Golden Tiara' make excellent edging plants or ground covers. Propagate by division.

Perovskia

A tall perennial for large-scale plantings or for use as a backdrop. With its finely cut gray foliage and long narrow spikes of translucent blue flowers, this plant creates a blue cloud effect. Full sun is a must or it will get too floppy. 'Blue Spires' is the best, most upright form. Growing to a height of 4 ft., this summer bloomer lasts and lasts. Hardy in Zones 5 to 9.

Lysimachia clethroides (Loosestrife, Gooseneck)

If you're looking to fill up an entire bed with just one plant, *Lysimachia* is a good choice. An aggressive plant that spreads by underground rhizomes, this plant is tough and definitely durable. A butterfly magnet, *Lysimachia* also makes an excellent cut flower. Reaching 2 to 3 in. tall, the white flowers provide an eye-popping display in July and August. Hardy in Zones 3 to 8 and a great plant for moist areas.

Phlox 'Bright Eyes' and 'Emerald' series

There's nothing quite like the sight of carpets of *Phlox subulata* in full bloom in April! This evergreen groundcover is only a few inches tall, with flowers that completely obscure the foliage. 'Emerald Blue' and 'Emerald Pink' are two fine varieties. Their creeping, matlike habit makes them perfect candidates for rock gardens or edging plants. Give this phlox plenty of sun and it will stick around for years to come. Hardy in Zones 2 to 9.

Lamium maculatum 'White Nancy', 'Beacon Silver'

Despite its unappealing common name of dead nettle, *Lamium* makes a wonderful groundcover for light shade. The silvery foliage is topped with white ('White Nancy', left), pink ('Beacon Silver', right), or mauve flowers, depending upon the cultivar you choose. Good drainage is essential for this spring-blooming plant. Plant it where it can hang over a retaining wall or cascade over rocks. Hardy in Zones 3 to 8.

Iris siberica (Siberian Iris)

These durable irises add a touch of class to any landscape. Their flowers rise above narrow leaves in June, creating a breathtaking display. It's hard to believe that a flower so dainty can be so easy to grow. Simply provide adequate moisture (they resent dry soils) and sun or part shade. The only hard part is deciding which variety to grow! It's a tough decision with so many fine colors to choose from, such as the purple 'Caesar's Brother', the white 'Snow Queen', or the lovely blue 'Tealwood'. Plants grow 18 to 36 in. tall and are hardy in Zones 4 to 8. Perfect for water gardens. Grow in full sun or part shade and propagate by division.

Rudbeckia 'Goldsturm'

Everyone knows and loves these cheerful yellow flowers with their black centers! A carefree perennial that blooms July through September, *Rudbeckia* in a large planting really puts on a show. Grow *Rudbeckia* in full sun and they will reach a height of 3 ft. Contrary to popular belief, they are not at all drought tolerant, so water during dry spells. Leave the seed heads standing after flowering to attract birds. Hardy in Zones 4 to 8. Propagate from seed or division.

Ornamental Grasses

These diverse plants are fast becoming popular in the U.S. Ranging from heights of just 6 in. to towering overhead at 10 ft. or more, grasses are available for every landscape situation. *Festuca* 'Elijah Blue' (next page, top center) is a charming little grass with icy blue leaves. Keep it in full sun and away from soggy soils, and it will thrive. Humid weather can cause it to die out, so use it only if your summers aren't too hot. It's

a good choice for edging beds, as it grows to only 12 in. Propagate by division. *Calamagrostis acutiflora* 'Stricta' (above, left), also called feather reed grass, is a narrow, clump grower that's one of the earliest grasses to bloom. The feathery flowers appear in July. It grows to 4 ft. and makes a perfect accent or exclamation point in the landscape. Grow it in sun or part shade. Hardy in Zones 6 to 9. Propagate by division. *Pennisetum* 'Hameln' (above, right), also called dwarf fountain grass, is a perfect clump grower for smaller landscapes. Hameln gets covered with narrow, bottle-brush flowers from July to frost. Full sun or part shade is best. Hardy in Zones 5 to 9.

Pulmonaria

Another good choice for the shade, *Pulmonaria* can be grown as a specimen or in masses. New cultivars are constantly being introduced and almost all have silver blotched leaves, making them attractive foliage plants. The flowers are blue, turning to pink. They appear in February and persist through April if the weather stays cool. Soil moisture must be maintained during the heat of the summer, but too much overhead irrigation will cause powdery mildew. If this occurs, cut back to the ground and fresh new leaves will emerge. Hardy in Zones 3 to 8. *Photo by Allan Armitage.*

Sedum

Sedum 'Autumn Joy' is the most commonly grown of all *Sedum*—and for good reason. Its succulent green leaves look great all season long, and the rosy pink flower heads deepen to bronze by fall. This a tall *Sedum*, growing to 3 ft. However, there are plenty of lesser-known stonecrops that are good, low groundcovers. These deserve more use in

landscapes, as they are fast growers, carefree, and evergreen. *Sedum* 'Weihenstephaner Gold' and *Sedum sexangulare* both have yellow flowers in June and are just a few inches tall. *Sedum* 'John Creech' makes a beautiful mat of shiny green leaves, accented by its pink flowers. All are hardy in Zones 2 to 9.

June 1998

Succeeding with Daylilies

Jim Nau

The grande dame of the perennial border, the daylily excels in performance across the U.S. While some perennials prefer coastal areas, others the heat of a Southern summer, and a few the chill of a Northern winter, daylilies cross all regions and climatic conditions, performing equally well regardless of the climate. Granted, there are extremes that even daylilies won't tolerate, but they're still one of the most versatile and widely distributed garden perennials.

Daylilies are hardy in Zones 4 to 9. In Zones 6 to 8, lilies with evergreen-variety foliage will be more persistent during the winter months. If you live in the upper regions of Zone 7 or in Zone 6, covering plants during extended cold weather may be advisable. The cold hardiness of roots, however, isn't in question. *Hemerocallis,* as a group, is very hardy and will return year after year.

Propagation

Daylilies are commonly propagated by division. Tissue-cultured plants are also available. Spring or fall is the time for digging and division. Most commercial sales are done on two-year-old plants. As you separate the clumps, divide the roots to have two to three shoots. Many commercially propagated pieces you'll receive will have one or two. Seed propagation is strictly for finding new cultivars and growing the species. Many times, however, the resulting plants are then replicated by either of the two methods noted. Occasionally, some references note that *Hemerocallis* is propagated by cuttings. Technically, cuttings taken from any of the species, or hybrids, won't root. Instead, small plantlets develop around stem bases. These can be removed, along with a root portion, to a propagation bench to fully root. It can take two to three years to get a strong flowering plant.

Germination Overview

Seed for the various species is available, although not readily found in the U.S. You can collect the seed yourself to try the methods below. Because you can readily propagate the various *Hemerocallis* selections by division, the following notes are provided only as a point of reference:

Sow the seed into an open flat and cover with a layer of propagation media (peat, vermiculite, mixtures, etc.), and keep media temperatures at 68 to 70°F. Germination starts in two to three weeks, but seedlings may appear in flushes ranging from two to seven weeks after sowing. If germination is slow, unusually erratic, or nonexistent, a cold/moist period may be of benefit. Sow seed in a peat-based media, cover as noted above, moisten, and store at 40°F for six weeks. Then germinate as above. Seed will germinate very irregularly over a period of three to eight weeks, and seedlings will need to be transplanted as they are ready—don't throw the tray away until germination is complete. From seed, plants will take two to three years to flower.

Growing On

From division: In August and September, *Hemerocallis* plants are dug, divided, and roots are immediately shipped to growers or stored. Commercial propagators will have roots available for shipping from late summer until early or midwinter. The roots can be potted up any time during this period for overwintering; developing plants can be sold the following spring. As for crop time, most varieties will be salable green between eight and ten weeks after potting up in gallons and growing on at 55°F nights. In general, divisions potted up in February and March will be rooted enough in the container to sell in May. These divisions will usually produce one to three active shoots. Obviously, the more shoots produced, the faster the plant will root and the quicker the crop time will be. Also, plants with three-stem bases will be more filled out than those that have only one. With one potting date, therefore, it's conceivable that salable plants, from a visual standpoint, will reach the same point over a two- or three-week period. *Hemerocallis,* like *Gladiolus,* usually grow in a one-sided formation. Instead of leaves positioning themselves all around the developing stem, the leaves are

two-ranked, opposite one another.
If there is only one active stem, the
plant won't appear visually full at
the time it's sold, especially if a
small root is potted to a gallon
pot. When using roots with one
shoot or if potting up dwarf varieties, you might try 2- or 3-qt.
containers—retail customers may
consider it a better value. A 4-qt.
pot will work better for larger-
growing varieties.

Hemerocallis varieties will
flower the first summer in the
garden if started early enough.
Plants overwintered from a fall
potting produce the best flowering plants the following summer; roots
potted up in March yield the least flowering plants. Dwarf varieties readily flower and can often be sold blooming in a gallon pot, even when the
division is potted up in March or April. Most sales are in April and May,
however, so allow eleven to fourteen weeks for flowering plants on
selected varieties when grown at 55°F nights. Sometimes varieties won't
flower at all and will develop a foliage canopy instead. In some cases, the
problem is that the plants are from one-year-old divisions and are too
small for flowering. Many growers pot these up into 2-gal. containers and
grow them on during the summer for fall or next spring sales. Granted,
this increases your costs and won't be applicable for everyone's business.

If roots are planted in the fall, make sure the plants have firmly rooted
before temperatures drop consistently below 40°F. Otherwise, 45°F
night temperatures are best to establish plants in pots before the onset
of cold weather. While cold hardy, daylilies need special care when
brought out of winter treatment to avoid root rots. Here in Chicago,
Hemerocallis plants can be brought out with limited problems when
night temperatures are still dropping below 40°F. If thawed out after
being overwintered in a cold frame, however, the bulbous roots are
susceptible to absorbing excess water and then bursting if allowed to
freeze again.

Varieties

Daylily varieties are often separated by their chromosome count. As you read through the various catalogs, notice the information on each plant's hybridization. Diploid daylilies have two sets of chromosomes with 3- to 6-in. blooms and softer colors. Tetraploid varieties have four sets of chromosomes, usually with a larger plant and flower size than the standard hybrids and often with frilled or ruffled petals. Tetraploids are usually more expensive but make a bigger, bolder show in the garden. Another class—miniature daylilies—is so-called due to their small flower size of 3-in. or less. While the flowers may be smaller, some varieties can grow as tall as 24 in.

Uses

In the daylily perennial border, little can match some of the larger types for arching habits and long-lasting color. Use as foundation plantings, massed outside the home, or as specimen plantings around the yard. *Hemerocallis* makes a good cut flower if you take a stem with open blooms and mixture of opened and opening flower buds, since the blooms generally last only day.

In the commercial landscape, daylilies work very well. A number of varieties will rebloom once initial flowering is over. In the interim, the foliage provides a softening and formal appearance of the planting. Daylilies are a welcome addition to any garden, providing bold and dramatic colors, especially yellow. The perennial border can literally dance with the vibrancy of these hues. Plant daylilies in a full-sun location, although they can tolerate partial shade. However, remember that *Hemerocallis* needs six hours of sunlight daily to produce strong stems and a profusion of flower color. Plant them where their foliage fountain of leaves can arch unhindered to the ground. Don't plant tight up against shrubs or large robust, herbaceous perennials. However, we've seen an excellent performance in our garden by combining them with upright, spiring plants that project through and above the foliage. Plants like *Lobelia cardinalis,* some of the dwarf *Delphinium* species, *Asphodeline lutea,* and other nonintrusive varieties combine well. Space plants 15 to 24 in. apart, depending on the variety, in a well-drained location. Soil pH should be between 6 and 7 for best performance. Plants don't require staking or any special treatment, but should be fed during the spring to encourage a strong bloom set.

They don't need regular division but, once planted, they can be lifted and separated every three or four years if you want to share plants with friends. Established clumps left undivided, however, can become robust (depending on the variety) and provide a dramatic background to your garden.

Editor's note: The author appreciates the time that Roy Klehm of Klehm Nursery, Champaign, Illinois, took to read and edit this information.

June 1998

Success with Butterfly Weed
Jim Nau

Asclepias tuberosa, also known as butterfly weed or butterfly flower, is a native perennial with one of the most vivid orange flowers available, though red and yellow colors are also common. The individual, crown-shaped blooms are ⅛ to ¼ in. across and form irregular clusters measuring 1 to 2 in. across. Butterflies are attracted to this plant's rich flower nectar. In late summer as the flowers fade, an elongated, tapered 4-in. seed pod develops from which seeds parachute to earth with silky, featherlike appendages.

Plants primarily grow upright, from 1½ to 2 ft. tall and spread 12 to 18 in. across. Their stems contain a white, milky sap that exudes when the plant is wounded or cut.

Asclepias is hardy in Zones 4 to 9 and flowers from June to August. The best flowering is in July, continuing for up to six weeks. Cut off the dead flower heads for additional color four weeks later.

Propagation
Seed and root cuttings are the most common ways to propagate. Divisions are possible but yield less reliable results, as the rootstocks are brittle and the plants are slow to emerge in spring.

Germination

Germination temperatures are 70 to 75°F. Seed can be covered or left exposed during germination.

Pretreatments: If seed is purchased during late fall or winter, it's most likely fresh seed. If germination is irregular or the percent of emerging seedlings low, moist-chill the seed for greater results.

Germination takes twenty-one to twenty-eight days, and transplanting can be done thirty-five to fifty-five days after sowing.

Growing On

From seed: Winter and early spring sowings will produce sporadically flowering plants the following summer. For full flowering and profusely blooming plants, however, sow seed the previous year, and transplant seedlings to quart containers by mid or late summer for overwintering. These containers can then be sold the following spring.

If you prefer pack sales, a mid-February sowing produces salable, green cell packs (32s) by mid-May when grown at 58°F night temperatures. Plants flower sporadically in mid to late July in the garden.

If plants are sown from seed during the winter, they should be grown warm (no less than 55°F nights) until they are sold in the spring, regardless of the container size. When winter-sown, plants grow erect with mostly one, sometimes two stems void of basal or side branches. If growth temperatures fall below 50°F for a period of time, plants will slow and the leaves may fall off.

I've grown this plant for years in our West Chicago gardens and have never seen the same performance as those that grow as weeds along Illinois roadsides. *Asclepias* hates transplanting, becoming weak and languid as the roots become bound into the container. For best performance, sow the seed into plug trays and transplant only once into a final container before planting into the garden.

Varieties

I'm not aware of any cultivated varieties of *A. tuberosa*. The orange variety is the most commonly offered varieties in the U.S. A mixture, 'Gay Butterflies', is available from seed and has orange, yellow, and red flowers on plants that grow to 3 ft. tall.

Uses

Asclepias is an excellent plant for the perennial border. As a cut flower, it performs well from two-year-old plantings, which have longer stems. Sear the cut area to prevent the sap from bleeding or oozing.

One additional point: Our plants suffer annually from an aphid infestation concentrated at the terminal 1 to 2 in. on each stem. If aphids are left unchecked, the plants will die out in two years.

September 1998

Which *Buddleia* Do Butterflies Like Best?

In trials at Clemson University, Clemson, South Carolina, researchers evaluated thirteen cultivars of *Buddleia davidii*, or butterfly bush, for flower color, nectar production, and visits by butterflies and moths to determine which are most appealing to the insects, *HortIdeas* reports.

In most cases, butterflies and moths were most attracted to cultivars with red, pink, or lavender-pink flowers and least attracted to cultivars with white or pale lavender flowers.

Throughout the season, 'Charming Summer', which has lavender-pink flowers; 'Royal Red', which has very deep pink flowers; 'Pink Delight, which has pink flowers; and 'Petite Plum', which has deep pink-purple flowers, attracted the most butterflies and moths. Cultivars that attracted fewer creatures included: 'Lochinich', which has pale lavender flowers; 'Black Knight', which has very deep purple flowers; 'Empire Blue', which as deep blue flowers; 'Nanho Blue', which has pale blue flowers; and 'Nanho Purple', which has pale blue-purple flowers. Those that attracted the fewest butterflies and moths were 'White Profusion' and 'White Bouquet', with white flowers; 'Opera', with pink flowers; and 'Dubonet', with blue flowers.

Researchers also found a less pronounced correlation between butterfly and moth attractiveness and nectar production. Cultivars that produced the most nectar included 'Charming Summer', 'Royal Red', 'Pink Delight', 'Lochinich', 'White Profusion', 'White Bouquet', and 'Opera'.

September 1998

Australian Perennial Culture Tips

Roger Elliot

Perennial production can be tricky, and their exploding popularity makes quality product essential for your customers. Try these tips for three top perennials.

Helichrysum

Helichrysum grows best in full sun with good drainage. It may need 30% shade in Sunbelt areas during summer. Overwatering creates problems, so keep soil barely moist. Use an acidic mix with a pH 5.5 to 6.5. Pinch at potting or within four weeks after potting. Prune no later than six to eight weeks before finish to avoid reducing the number of flowers. Plants are ready for sale twelve to sixteen weeks after plugs or liners are potted.

Maintaining very compact growth, 'Nullarbor Gold 'N' Bronze' *Helichrysum* has foliage that rarely gets taller than 1 ft. Plants can spread to 3 ft. across after two years. Plants flower throughout the year, peaking during spring, summer, and early fall. Flower heads are 2 to 3 in. across, held on slender stems above narrow, bright green leaves. Buds are pale to mid-bronze, opening to reveal numerous bright golden yellow papery petal-like bracts and a golden disc. Use it in baskets and 4-in., 6-in., or 1-gal. pots.

Brachycome

Brachycome usually grows best in soils that don't dry out too readily, but it dislikes waterlogging. It prefers sun or partial shade and may need 30% shade in the Sunbelt during summer. *Brachycome* likes soils with pH 5.5 to 6.5 in a free-draining, well-aerated media. Plants grow well in areas that don't have heavy frosts, though they can handle temperatures down to 25°F without too much damage. Liners or

Brachycome 'Billabong Bright Eyes'

plugs should have at least four main breaks at potting, and after another four weeks, shear plants to about 2 in. above media.

Dwarf and compact with finely lobed bright green leaves, *Brachycome* 'Billabong Bright Eyes' has ½-in. mauve-blue flowers. Plants in 6-in. pots are salable eight to twelve weeks after potting. It can sucker lightly as it develops to 6 in. tall and may spread to 3 ft. across. Use in mass plantings, 4-in., 6-in., or 1-gal. pots or baskets. The main selling window is from March to November, but some nurseries find they can extend their selling window.

Scaevola

Scaevola prefers sun or partial shade. Grow these plants under cover if frost is likely, but compact plants are more likely if grown outdoors. Keep night temperatures from 35 to 75°F inside to promote compactness. Plants may require 30% shade in the Sunbelt during summer. Light applications of low phosphorus fertilizers are beneficial, but be careful not to force-feed plants because this promotes foliage at the expense of flowers. Good liners should have three to four main breaks at potting. Pinch back to 1 in. above previous breaks at potting or within four weeks of potting. You can pinch or shear lightly any time except within eight to ten weeks of finish.

June 1996

Hosta Culture Tips

Jim Nau

With the large number of hosta varieties available, it's difficult to pinpoint the best techniques for growing quality crops. Here are some tips for growing and finishing this top perennial shade performer.

Bareroot plants are readily available for either fall or winter shipping, depending on the variety. These varieties can be a species or represent hybrid crosses or sports (mutations), and crop times will differ. Therefore, it's difficult to give a general crop time for all hosta cultivars. However, if potted in 1-gal. containers, most varieties will be salable in seven to nine weeks for roots potted up in late February and March and grown at 55 to 58°F nights, with days warmer by 8 to 15°F. For larger plants as well as the slower growing varieties used as borders or edging, allow eight to eleven weeks in a 3- to 4-qt. pot and the same night temperatures.

Tissue-cultured plants are often sold in liners or trays of seventy-two plants per flat. If potted up into 1-qt. pots, they'll finish off in five to eight weeks, depending on the variety. Grow on at 55 to 58°F nights.

If your goal is to have a plant with limited leaf number (usually less than eight) with a "just rooted" rootball, then these crop times and temperatures will suit your needs. If you're looking for a well-rooted plant with full, lush foliage, you'll need to add two more weeks to the crop time above and four more weeks for more compact or slower-growing varieties. Or better yet, pot up your divisions or transplants in the autumn and overwinter dormant for spring sales.

Crop times are based on a quick turnover rate for mass merchandising. If you can afford the time and labor, give plants some additional time to improve their appearance.

November 1996

Perennial Success: Quality *Clematis* Every Time

Rob Wein

Clematis can be a profitable crop and is relatively easy to finish from a liner if you follow a few guidelines.

Media: A well-drained soil is essential. We recommend a peat lite media. Maintain a pH of 5.7 to 6.2.

Fertility: A constant feed of 200 ppm nitrogen is ideal. Monitor soluble salts, and leach if necessary. Although liquid feed provides more flexibility, you can also use slow-release fertilizers effectively.

Heat: Ideally, keep plants in a nearly frost-free environment through winter. *Clematis* requires extended periods of below 50°F to begin dormancy. Dormancy should last at least six weeks. Following dormancy, you can grow plants with little or no heat unless additional root development and top growth are required. If so, grow at 55°F night temperature and gradually reduce heat three to four weeks before shipping to "harden off" your crop. Venting should start at 75F.

Irrigate carefully: Only water plants when you can't squeeze any moisture out of the media. At this time, water thoroughly even if you need two irrigations to saturate the soil. Be aware that different cultivars dry out at different rates, so spot watering may be necessary.

Planting: Plant liners so the crown is buried at least 1 in. below the soil level. Unless your liner is dormant, remove bottom leaves before transplanting.

Density and maintenance: For optimum returns per square foot, grow your crop pot tight. Keep plants twisted to the stake or steered. Otherwise, matting will occur, and fungi will have an opportunity to invade.

Maintain good sanitation: Start clean by purchasing *Clematis* liners from a reputable supplier. Use clean or pasteurized soil. Let your supplier recommend a preventative fungicide program.

August 1996

Trachelium Production Tricks

Trachelium caeruleum, or throatwort, has become a popular cut flower that's used as filler in bouquets. Its panicle flowers come in striking lavender and dark blue as well as creamy white and pastel pink. Most growers purchase plugs rather than propagate this tender perennial. Here are some cultural tips from Vegmo Plant, Rijsenhout, the Netherlands.

Trachelium are easily started from plug seedlings and may be greenhouse-grown in containers or field-grown in ground beds. *Trachelium* seed germinates in five to seven days at 65 to 68°F. Leave seed exposed to light for germination. Keep seed and seedling trays under short days to prevent premature flowering.

Crop time varies from ten weeks for July plantings to seventeen weeks for November through January plantings. Plant out at a density of fifty-four plants per sq. yd. for single-stem production, eighteen plants per sq. yd. for pinched production.

Trachelium 'Lake Tahoe'

Lighting

Long days encourage flowering; short days inhibit it. Provide continuous sixteen-hour days, or use night interruption lighting (mum lighting). Light at an intensity of 15 watts per m². Light until harvest to avoid misshapen, pyramidal flowers.

HID lights will make plants flower faster; incandescent lighting will promote faster growth.

For crops planted from the end of May until early July, encourage vegetative growth before initiating flowers by applying short days (twelve hours) during weeks 2 and 4. The exact length of short-day treatment depends on light levels and temperatures.

Temperature

Trachelium is native to the Mediterranean and prefers cooler temperatures. Therefore, it doesn't do well outdoors in the hot summers of the South or Midwest. For fall and winter crops, grow at 50 to 52°F for the first three weeks, then raise night temperatures to 58°F and days to 60°F. Spring crops can be grown at 60°F nights and 62 to 68°F days. In colder climates, additional heat may be necessary to maintain 52°F nights and 62°F days. Note: While warmer temperatures will speed up flowering, they may also cause poor flower quality and thin stems.

Fertilization

Plants require average fertility. During bud formation, apply additional potassium nitrate. Be sure to rinse off plants afterward to avoid burning. Don't use ammonium fertilizers on *Trachelium*.

Also, *Trachelium* is very sensitive to high manganese levels in the soil. Use care when steaming, as steam releases manganese bound in the soil, which can result in manganese toxicity. Toxicity symptoms will show as leaf damage during the last stage of development. Steaming for four hours or less and using iron chelate prevents leaf damage. Apply iron chelate three to five weeks after planting.

Postharvest

Harvest flowers when a quarter to a third of panicles are three-quarters open. Flowers normally have a ten-day to two-week vase life in water. Silver thiosulfate can improve keeping quality. Store stems in water for twenty-four hours at 39°F before shipping.

September 1997

Producing Israel's Unique Protea

Danziger Dan Flower Farm

The Proteaceae family is one of the oldest and lowest in terms of genetic development. About 75 genera and 1,350 species of small trees and shrubs commonly found in Australia and South Africa make up the family. Proteas have high value as flowering pot plants, bedding plants, cut flowers (fresh and dried), and fruit trees (macadamia is in the Proteaceae family). They are mainly characterized by their evergreen nature, long flowering period of several months, and favorable flowering time (fall, winter, and the beginning of spring).

Though Europe has been the traditional protea market, in recent years, two markets—the U.S. and Japan—have expanded significantly. The worldwide market can still absorb large quantities of proteas without lowering prices, according to a recent study by the Israel Ministry of Agriculture. Still, the market is in need of new varieties to refresh existing selections.

Proteas are commercially grown primarily in the Southern Hemisphere and are found as commercial cut flowers in New Zealand,

Australia, South Africa, Hawaii, and Zimbabwe. Outdoor production has also increased in the Northern Hemisphere. Here are some tips for successfully producing these unusual and increasingly popular plants.

Growing Conditions

Optimal climatic conditions for protea production are those prevailing in the temperate Mediterranean zones. Most proteas grow outside in full sun, but not in extremely high temperatures. Pruning can be done right after flowering, toward spring.

Soil is a more crucial factor; proteas usually prefer acidic soil with a 5.5 to 7.0 pH. However, some of the genera and species can be successfully grown with higher pH levels.

In Israel, *Leucadendron* is a very popular genus with a wide range of species. If you have alkaline soil, as in Israel, one way to keep pH down is to plant proteas on small mounds while keeping pH levels below 7.0 by adding sulfuric acid during the first year of production. Another strategy is to graft varieties on root stocks resistant to high pH, excess phosphorus, and soil problems such as *Phytophthora* and nematodes. Grafting allows protea production in most types of soil in Israel, as long as they're well drained and have good airflow.

Proteas have two root systems: the usual roots for support and absorption and proteoid roots, which is a root system composed of lumps of small short-lived roots located close to the surface. As these roots are very efficient in absorbing minerals, any excess quantity is easily absorbed and may kill the plant.

Preplanting

As cut flowers grown in the open field, proteas require minimal planting preparation. There is no need for special structures such as greenhouses or shade houses. Buying plants is the main investment, but they are perennial stock, which can yield for at least ten years.

Harvest and Postharvest

Unlike plants such as carnations, chrysanthemums, and roses, proteas can be harvested over a long period of time at different stages of development. They can be harvested for a variety of uses (single, spray, or with flowers or greens). This means harvest time is flexible.

After harvest, machinery may be used for bunching and packing. Proteas have a long vase life—so long, in fact, that proteas can be exported from Israel by sea, rather than by air, significantly reducing overall costs.

Pests

Few pests and diseases attack proteas; therefore, spraying is usually minimal.

December 1997

Sow and Grow Right with These
Bread-and-Butter Perennials

Monarda and salvia are considered must-haves for the summer garden (and fall garden, in the case of salvia) by perennial enthusiasts everywhere. Here's what Jim Nau of Ball Seed suggests for top performance.

Monarda

Monarda, commonly known as bee balm, usually isn't grown from seed. Instead, all of the named cultivars, with the exception of 'Panorama Mix', are propagated primarily from cuttings. If you're interested in growing from seed, you can expect *Monarda* to grow quickly with 55°F nights, with an eight to ten week green sale time in 32-cell packs. Plants are hardy and will take cooler temperatures from 48 to 58°F with little problem, although they will grow more slowly at the cooler temperatures. Plants won't flower the same year from seed if started in January or later.

Seed-propagated varieties will vary in height, darkness of foliage and flower color, and even shades of a single color. Also, an unusual trait of seed-propagated varieties is that they won't have any powdery mildew in the first year after sowing. However, the following year the plants will flower readily and will be covered in powdery mildew. Growing from seed helps breeders select new varieties, but because of the powdery mildew problem, it does a disservice to the crop (and home gardeners) when the crop is sold commercially.

Salvia

Salvia superba is an easy perennial crop to grow from seed and is one of the few perennials that can be sown from January to early March, producing sizeable plants by May that will flower during the summer that first year. The flower power is much better the second year after sowing, but is still respectable the first year from seed.

Salvia pratensis won't flower the same year, if seed is sown any time during the winter or spring, despite production of rapid growing rosettes. If February-sown seed is treated like a bedding plant and is transplanted to the garden from a cell pack in early spring, *Salvia pratensis* will grow 4 to 5 in. tall and spread to 24 in. wide.

If flowering plants are preferred, sow seed the summer prior to desired sales and transplant to quart or gallon containers for overwintering. Many crops are offered by commercial propagators in a wide range of plug or liner sizes already vernalized, but this is virtually unheard of in the case of *Salvia pratensis*.

A Guide to Grow On

	Germination Percentage	Seed for 1,000 Plants (oz.)	Number of Seeds (oz.)	Germination Temperature	Lighting	Days to Germinate	Days Sowing to Transplant	Growing on Temperature	Crop Time (Weeks)
Monarda	70–85	½₂	56,000/oz.	70–72°F	Cover lightly	5–8	20–28	55°F	8–10
Salvia pratensis	60–70	¹∕₁₆	28,350/oz.	70°F	Cover lightly	4–6	15–22	55–58°F	9–10
Salvia superba	75–85	¹∕₁₆	25,000/oz.	72°F	Light or cover	4–8	15–22	50–55°F	9–11

	Number of Plants Qt./.95 L. Gal./3.8 L.		Blooming Months	Hardiness Zones	Garden Height	Garden Spacing	Staking	Location	
Monarda	1	1	June–August	4–9	3 ft.	12–18 in.	No	Full sun	
Salvia pratensis	1	1	July–August	3–7	12–32 in.	24 in	No	Full sun	
Salvia superba	1	1	May–June	4–8	15–24 in.	10 in.	No	Full sun	❏

April 1999

Cut Flower Perennials from Seed

Jeff McGrew

There are many perennials that lend themselves for use as cut flowers; a few are world-class and are produced professionally for the cut flower market worldwide.

Choosing the Correct Perennial

What makes a perennial a good cut flower? Vase life is one of the most important qualities to consider; stem length and flower presentation on the stem are other critical factors. There are also economic points, such as flower production per plant and return per square foot of growing space (per production period), that must be considered.

Growing climate must also be considered, since environmental factors greatly influence perennial cut flower quality. Can the variety in question receive adequate vernalization or dormancy period to ensure proper flower induction, initiation, and development? Many growing environments are marginal or simply not suited for the production of quality flowers demanded by today's marketplace.

Given these considerations, here are a few perennials that make great cut flowers. All are started from seed and have proven themselves reliable sellers in most wholesale cut flower markets.

Delphinium x *belladonna* hybrids

The delphinium group is a large and important one. *Delphinium consolida* is an annual commonly called larkspur delphinium. It's one of the top performers for both the fresh cut and dried flower industries. The so-called delphinium hybrid group (*Delphinium* x *cultorum*) contains the large double-flowered types (mostly hardy perennials) called the Giant Pacific hybrids. These cultivars account for 30 to 40% of the delphinium cut flower market. The *Delphinium belladonna* types are also perennial, and they account for about 6% of the delphinium cut market. Belladonna types have large, single flowers arranged symmetrically on 12- to 16-in. stems. Colors can range from dark blue (sometimes called *D. bellamosum*), light blue (called *D.* x *belladonna* or 'Clivedon Beauty') and a pure white. Of the belladonna types, the dark blue varieties have a larger market share than the whites or light blues.

In general, delphiniums appreciate cooler growing temperatures—nights 45 to 55°F and days 60 to 80°F. Delphiniums can be profitably grown in open field or greenhouse conditions.

For greenhouse forcing, transplant a seven- to ten-week-old plug seedling into a cool greenhouse between October and March. Maintain cool night temperatures (45 to 55°F) during the early production period (first six to eight weeks after transplanting)—this will maximize flowering potential. Total crop time ranges from ten to fourteen weeks (after transplant), depending on planting time and production temperature. If properly grown, two to three flower flushes can be achieved in one season. Two support wires are recommended. Space plants 10 in. on center. Drip irrigation, not overhead watering, is recommended.

Outdoor field growing is the most common production method. Transplants are put out August through October or March to April. In cold growing areas, protect the young transplants from freezing temperatures with row cover cloth. Space plants 8 to 10 in. apart. Support wire is also recommended for outside production along with drip or bottom irrigation practices. In northern growing environments, one to two flower flushes are normal. In a more moderate growing area, two to three flushes are possible.

Harvest the flower stem when 20 to 30% of the individual flowers are open. Use a bactericide and an ethylene inhibitor (like STS) to prevent petal shattering and reduced vase life.

Limonium gmelinii (Siberian Statice)

This very winter-hardy perennial is a native of Eastern Europe and Russia—particularly Siberia. Siberian statice does best in a growing environment with moderate to low summer humidity levels; the winters must also have night temperatures near freezing for at least a few weeks. This winter chilling maximizes the following summer's flower production. In warm and temperate growing areas, Siberian statice might bloom poorly or not at all.

The flower stems are round and smooth (no leaves or foliage are on the flowering stems) and can reach 20 in. tall. The flowers are lilac-blue in color and consist of a number of small flowers or florets grouped on the top portion of the stem. When conditions are right, this statice can produce economically for several years, with multiple flowering stems expected on older, mature plants. Well-drained soil is important for long-term production.

Harvest stems of *Limonium gmelinii* when 60 to 70% of the florets are open. Siberian statice can be used in either dried or fresh arrangements. *Photo by Kieft Flowerseeds.*

Siberian statice is grown almost exclusively as a field crop. Recommended spacings are 12 in. by 16 in. A field support wire is not often used unless conditions are very windy or subject to occasional high rainfall.

Limonium gmelinii is used in fresh and dry flower production. Flowering stems should be harvested when 60 to 70% of the florets are open. A bactericide is used in the postharvest care of the flower. Flowering normally occurs in July or August. Only one flower flush can be expected per year.

Aquilegia vulgaris 'Barlow' Series

This unusual columbine is different from other *Aquilegia* because it produces fully double, spurless flowers; a high percentage of flowers face outward (not hanging down). These characteristics have improved Barlow's vase life and reduced its propensity for shattering. This series is also now available for the first time in straight colors.

Transplant eight- to nine-week plants at a spacing of 12 in. on center. These plants generally will not flower that same year from sowing, but the following spring they will give three to five flower stems, 30 to 40 in. long. The second and consequent years can yield five to ten stems per plant per year. Support wire is recommended. A well-drained soil with a pH of 5.8 to 6.8 is best. It is important that *Aquilegia* 'Barlow' is produced in a climate where winter night temperatures drop to at least 50°F for six to eight weeks. Poor winter vernalization can result in reduced flower production.

Proper postharvest care is also important. Use a bactericide and ethylene inhibitor plus a water surfactant to help fluids move up the long stem.

Campanula persicifolia

Commonly called peach leaf bellflower, it produces non-branching stems normally between 24 in. and 40 in. long with 1- to 1½-in. wide bell-shaped flowers formed along the stem. Flower colors are light blue, white ('Alba'), and 'Telham Beauty' ('China Blue').

Campanula persicifolia thrives and produces its best quality flowers when growing temperatures are moderate and when cool nights persist. Night temperatures below 60°F and days below 85°F will produce strong stems and flowers. Warm nights and hot days will develop thin, weak flowering stems.

This campanula also demands a fairly cold winter vernalization period so proper flower initiation can occur; ten or twelve weeks at 40°F is the minimum requirement. *C. persicifolia* can flower under short-day conditions (if cold requirement is met), but longer days of fourteen to sixteen hours improve the stem length and reduce time to flower.

A spacing of 12 in. between plants is good for a perennial field planting. Provide a balanced fertility regime, but keep nitrogen levels below 100 ppm. Wire supports will help keep stems straight.

Divided plants can be artificially cooled (refrigerated) for twelve weeks at 40°F. These vernalized divided plants can be forced in a cool greenhouse or planted outside if conditions are right. Flowering will occur in eight to twelve weeks when night temperatures are between 50 and 58°F. Stems are ready to cut when one to two flowers are open and buds are swollen. A postharvest bactericide is also recommended.

Campanula persicifolia thrives and produces its best quality flowers when daytime growing temperatures are moderate and nights are cool.
Photo by Kieft Flowerseeds.

Scabiosa caucasica

This species of *Scabiosa* is fairly hardy (USDA Zones 3 to 7), but is also a first-year blooming perennial (sow to flower) when planted out early in the season and put into a growing environment with naturally cool nights of 60°F or less.

Scabiosa caucasica produces a blue-green foliage base with stems of 20 in. to 24 in. long. The beautiful flowers are fairly flat in shape, 3 to 4 in. in diameter with a white to yellow center. Colors include pure white and shades of blue and lavender. The 'Perfects' series offers good cultivars, and a variety called 'Fama' has large lavender-blue flowers and is also very popular for cutting. Flowering normally occurs in midsummer in northern environments and earlier in warmer growing areas. Warm conditions for a prolonged period will stop or slow flower production. A field spacing of 10 in. between plants is recommended.

A support wire is important to keeps stems upright. Harvest flowers when 40 to 50% of the center disk flowers are open. Use a postharvest bactericide after cutting.

Rudbeckia Variety Review

Jim Nau

Rudbeckia hirta is an excellent perennial for well-drained areas in full-sun locations. *Rudbeckia* is often treated as an annual in the Midwest or in any area where the fall can be cold and wet. It doesn't appreciate overly moist conditions, and dwarf varieties often die from foliar diseases brought on by excessive moisture in combination with high humidity, such as powdery mildew. Plants flower readily from seed the first season, and varieties such as 'Marmalade', 'Goldilocks', 'Becky Mix', and 'Toto' will even flower well in pots or packs.

Rudbeckia germinates in five to ten days at 70°F. The seed can be lightly covered during germination. For flowering 4-in. pots in May, sow in January, and use one plant per pot. For taller varieties, allow eleven to fifteen weeks for green packs.

Among varieties, both 'Marmalade' and 'Goldilocks' are dwarf selections that grow to only 15 in. tall in the garden. Marmalade does have problems with powdery mildew, but provides color from planting until August. Flowers are single, up to 3 in. across, in a golden yellow to light orange color.

'Goldilocks', which flowers ten days earlier, is a semidouble- to double-flowering variety that grows to 12 in. tall in the garden. Flowers range from 3 to 4 in. across, and the variety is excellent in packs or pots.

'Becky Mix' is a simple mix with two predominant flower colors—orange and orange red. Occasionally, a golden-yellow color pops up. Becky is a pot plant variety growing only 10 in. tall in the pot and 12 to 14 in. tall in the garden. Flowers are single and are 2½ to 3½ in. across.

'Indian Summer' is an All-America Selections award winner with huge, 5- to 9-in., single to semidouble golden-orange flowers on plants 30 to 36 in. tall.

In the taller varieties, 'Double Gold' is of particular value for cutting or as a background plant in the garden. 'Double Gold' has double flowers up to 6 in. across in a stable color of golden orange.

September 1997

Perennial Success: *Rudbeckia*

Tim Brindley

When people talk about *Rudbeckia*, they normally think of 'Goldsturm', the Perennial Plant of the Year for 1999. An excellent grower and a mainstay in any perennial garden, black-eyed Susan (as it is commonly known) is a wonderful hardy perennial with vivid color.

But don't stop there. The past few years have seen the popularity increase on some "soft" perennial varieties such as 'Becky Mix', 'Sonora', 'Toto', and 'Goldilocks' (hirta varieties). These beautiful, easy-to-grow varieties have brought a new twist to the *Rudbeckia* marketing scheme and are great additions to your growing programs.

Following is a "steps for success" process that most growers can follow to bring extra profits and additional sales to their business.

Propagation

When producing *Rudbeckia*, all you need is a little time. The following procedures are proven in our operation and should help you in your planning and growing.

'Goldsturm': Moist—chill seeds for two to four weeks at 40°F. Sow into 72 plug cells. The first several days are crucial. You must keep temperatures at 70°F in greenhouses and mist six seconds every five minutes the first two days. Day three, mist six seconds every ten minutes until germination begins. After germination begins, mist six seconds every eighteen minutes until germination is complete.

Hirta varieties ('Becky Mix', 'Sonora', 'Toto', and 'Goldilocks'): Follow the same procedures, but do not pretreat seeds.

It's very important during the germination process to constantly evaluate your seeds. Some will come on faster than others, and the misting days and times may vary from time to time. We suggest touring every three hours after day one to ensure proper misting is occurring.

Transplanting and Growing

Transplanting *Rudbeckia* is a basic process. I suggest dislodging plugs before transplanting, which will keep the foliage in good condition. One plant per 1-gal. pot is sufficient and produces a beautiful, full plant.

Grow these plants outside in the spring, summer, and fall with minimal spacing (two to three inches). Grow in direct sunlight, as *Rudbeckia* thrive on warm weather and a lot of natural light.

Growing time in the spring and summer is usually six to eight weeks to finish, depending on temperatures. Flowering usually begins about the sixth week. Minimal cleaning is required if you turn your product quickly. The growth pattern is quick; be sure to spread your crops out at two-week intervals to achieve best plants and turns.

Fertilization and Water Needs

All our *Rudbeckia* are grown outdoors. We water overhead with sprinklers set at 30-ft. spacing. Fertilizer is used and incorporated into the irrigation process two to three times a week in spring and summer months, maybe up to five times a week. Our media also has a slow-release, 120-day Osmocote incorporated. Our media is a bark or peanut hull mix with minor elements. "Hot" soil can be a problem with *Rudbeckia*. Be sure your soil temperature isn't above 80°F. "Hot" soil can and will damage the roots of these tender plugs.

Growth Regulators

To control the height of *Rudbeckia,* I suggest applying Bonzi at 40 ppm as needed. It is still undecided as to how much Bonzi helps on *Rudbeckia,* so as an alternate measure, Sumagic at 20 ppm may be a better application. Of course, the best growth regulator is sales, so sell your *Rudbeckia* at its prime height.

Pest and Disease Control

Factor is applied as an herbicide to prevent weeds in the container (one pound of Factor per acre two times per season). When using Factor, be sure roots are well established and reaching for the bottom of the container. Disease problems have been almost nonexistent for us so far.

Conclusion

Now that you have a formula to follow and some helpful hints, your *Rudbeckia* crops should yield you great success and profits. Remember that black-eyed Susans are an old perennial favorite and a proven addition to any garden. Take advantage of any promotional opportunities you can. Use innovative tags, be aggressive, and be prepared. Then you will be profitable.

April 1999

'99 Perennial of the Year Doesn't Need Cold to Flower

Recommendations for controlling flowering in *Rudbeckia* 'Goldsturm', the Perennial Plant Association's 1999 Perennial of the Year, are available for the first time. At Michigan State University (MSU), Lansing, Michigan, the team of Erik S. Runkle, Royal D. Heins, Arthur C. Cameron, and William H. Carlson discovered that 'Goldsturm' doesn't require a cold treatment to flower, though it does speed up the time to flower by 35%. They found that under long days, a fifteen-week treatment at 41°F increases flowering speed by four weeks when grown at 68°F but provides no other benefits.

Cold treatments reduced the number of new nodes below the first inflorescence, but didn't affect flowering percentage or uniformity, flower number, plant height, or vigor.

Like many *Rudbeckia,* 'Goldsturm' is a long-day plant regardless of cold treatment. In the MSU studies, both cooled and noncooled plants had a thirteen- to fourteen-hour photoperiod.

Noncooled plants under thirteen-hour photoperiods developed larger, more vertically oriented leaves than plants under shorter day lengths. Researchers recommend growing 'Goldsturm' under approximate thirteen-hour photoperiods to promote vegetative growth until plants have at least ten nodes. To induce flowering, provide a fourteen-hour inductive photoperiod without cold treatment, a thirteen-hour photoperiod following cold treatment, or a four-hour night interruption.

Interestingly, the researchers found that plants under inductive photoperiods developed at a 13% faster rate before cold treatment. The difference can't be attributed to temperature or light levels, as conditions measured before and after cold treatment were similar. This contrasts the tendencies of perennials like *Phlox paniculata* that develop nodes faster and are more vigorous after cold treatment.

April 1999

Start Your Garden Mums off Right

For top-quality garden mums, plant your cuttings as soon as you receive them, recommends Van Zanten North America, Oxnard, California. If you can't plant them immediately, you can store them for several days in a cooler at 37 to 42°F. But before placing them in a cooler, inspect them for damage from heating, freezing, breakage, or dehydration.

Always plant cuttings into moist media. Planting into dry media is a sure way to reduce cuttings' initial growth and future potential. Place them only deep enough to just cover the roots. In some instances, planting too deeply may result in retarded growth, aid in disease development, and even cause death.

Water plants thoroughly immediately after planting. Allowing garden mum cuttings to wilt can inhibit their takeoff, future branching potential, and overall growth. It's beneficial to mist or syringe plants frequently for the first few days or until plants are fully turgid and roots are actively taking up water.

Three to five days after planting, when cuttings are fully turgid, give a hard pinch. This will force out lower breaks, which tend to be more vegetative.

Providing liquid feed one week after planting helps plants get off to a vigorous start, and rooted garden mum cuttings can use liquid fertilizer from the moment they're planted. Use a 200- to 300-ppm fertilizer solution of nitrogen, phosphorus, and potassium to water in plants.

Garden mums are very reproductive and have six- to seven-week response times. But they aren't entirely photoresponsive and may set bud regardless of the number of hours they're lighted.

To prevent garden mum cuttings from becoming prematurely reproductive or budded, keep them actively growing. Anything that slows or stops plants' growth may push them into bud. Provide optimum moisture and fertilizer and monitor temperatures. Several cool nights in a row can initiate buds prematurely. Pinching off these buds and providing proper moisture and fertilizer allows plants to continue to grow and develop.

June 1999

Spice up Your Herbs with Oregano

Conrad Richter

Oregano is one of the most popular herbs in the garden center trade. In demand for its hot, spicy flavor, the "pizza herb" is a quick crop from seed and an easy sale provided you start with the right varieties.

The trouble is that for years the seed industry, out of ignorance, has sold the wrong seeds as oregano. Usually seeds of a plant that is more correctly called common marjoram—a hardy perennial with slightly hairy leaves and pinkish flowers—are offered as oregano. Common marjoram (not to be confused with sweet marjoram, *Origanum majorana,* an entirely different herb with its own distinct flavor and uses) has the right botanical name, *Origanum vulgare,* but none of the typical flavor and aroma of the imported dried product used in Greek and Italian cooking. Selling the common marjoram variety as oregano is a major disappointment for customers because the taste is totally insipid, hardly better than eating grass, and the leaves have little or no aroma. Sometimes a completely different herb, summer savory, *Satureja hortensis,* masquerades as oregano in garden centers. When discerning customers find such mislabeled or inferior material sold as oregano, they go somewhere else.

Although there are many varieties of aromatic oreganos, including types from Syria, Turkey, Mexico, and elsewhere, by far the variety most readily adapted for commercial pot and pack sales is Greek oregano, *Origanum vulgare hirtum.* The other regional and specialty varieties are rarely found in the horticultural trade because seed supplies are lacking, requiring more costly, labor-intensive propagation by cuttings. Of the truly aromatic oreganos, the Greek variety is the only one for which seeds are available in commercial quantities.

The leaves of the Greek oregano are somewhat hairy, and the flowers are white instead of pink. It's a perennial, surprisingly hardy to Zone 4, which is much cooler than its native Greece. Because it yields a harvest of fresh or dried tops the first season, Greek oregano can also be sold in packs with spring annuals.

The spring season is the main market opportunity for oregano. Typically seeds are started, grown, and marketed in much the same way as annual bedding plants. Oregano is also grown for the fresh-cut herb market in greenhouses usually equipped with hydroponic systems. This segment of the industry is still very small, but there is increasing interest.

Propagation

Greek oregano can be sown in a variety of plug trays, from a 128 to a 288 tray or broadcast into seed flats. Larger growers are sowing direct in packs or in 3- or 3½-in. pots to minimize labor cost. Plugs transplanted to 4-in. pots will yield a superior product of consistent size, but the added cost of transplanting is an important consideration.

Sowing

The sowing medium should be a lightly fertilized peat with 20% perlite added to improve drainage. The pH should be 5 to 7. Watering trays before seeding ensures even moisture down the trays and facilitates easy watering after sowing without washing out seeds or seed cover. One gram of seed contains 4,500 seeds. Typical germination rates are between 60 to 75%. Each plug should get between five and ten seeds; direct-seeded packs should get ten to fifteen seeds per cell; and direct-seeded pots should get fifteen to twenty seeds sown near the pot centers. After sowing, cover lightly with fine vermiculite.

Germination

Optimal temperature for germination is 72 to 77°F. After the initial watering under mist, trays should be kept evenly moist but not saturated with water, and humidity should be 85%. Germination occurs in seven to fourteen days. Light levels can be at ambient greenhouse levels throughout the germination and growing on stages. If a germination chamber is used, light isn't required to promote germination, but enough light is needed to prevent seedlings from stretching until the trays are moved to the greenhouse.

As seedlings become established, reduce the temperature to 64 to 72°F, and humidity to 70 to 75%, and ensure that ventilation is adequate to prevent damping off. Half-strength feedings of 50 to 75 ppm nitrogen can be applied after seedlings are established. It takes four to six weeks for plugs to reach transplanting size.

Growing On

Greek oregano takes ten to twelve weeks from seed to plug to finished 4-in. pots. Direct-sowing in packs and in 3- or 3½-in. pots takes eight to ten weeks to get marketable product from seed. The precise timing of the crop is not critical because flowering is not required or even desired. The objective is to produce plants with compact masses of well-formed leaves.

Transplanting

Plugs should be transplanted at the four- to six-week stage, when seedlings have at least four pairs of true leaves. Avoid allowing plugs from getting root bound, delaying growth; however, if crop timing is off, even root-bound plugs will grow on to produce a marketable crop.

Potting Soil

Like most herbs of Mediterranean origin, Greek oregano requires good drainage. Peat-based soils require 20% perlite to ensure adequate drainage. Some growers are using custom compost-based mixes with sand and perlite for the "organically grown" market. For active growth, the minimum nighttime temperature is 46°F, and the minimum daytime temperature is 59°F. Daytime temperatures over 86°F will slow growth. A regime of 64 to 72°F daytime and 59 to 64°F nighttime will produce sturdy, compact plants. Humidity shouldn't exceed 75%, and exposure should be full direct sun. Supplementary lighting isn't required except in far northern areas where the daylength is less than ten hours.

Like many Mediterranean herbs, oregano prefers conditions somewhat on the dry side. Overwatering will stunt growth and cause root rot.

Fertilization

In peat-based potting soils, regular feedings should build from 50 to 100 ppm with a complete fertilizer. Compost-based mixes usually don't require supplemental feeding before sale.

Pests and Diseases

Whitefly, spider mites, aphids, and thrips attack oregano, and because herbs are edible plants, few controls are available when pest outbreaks occur. The first line of defense is close monitoring of pest populations. Thorough weekly examination of crops with the aid of yellow and blue sticky traps will identify outbreaks at the earliest stages, when contact pesticides such as Safer's insecticidal soap are most effective. Relatively little-known products suitable for application on edible plants have been introduced in the past five to ten years, such as neem-based sprays (e.g., Neemazad), fungus-based controls (e.g., Naturalis-O), and others. These may be useful on herbs, although they're usually slower acting than contact sprays and may not provide effective control on a fast crop like oregano. Beneficials such as whitefly parasites and mite predators aren't effective on fast crops such as oregano. Thorough spot spraying with contact sprays at the earliest stages of pest infestation has given the best results. Mildew occurs when temperatures are low, air circulation is poor, and water is allowed to remain on leaves at night, but with care, mildew is rarely a problem.

With the right variety, oregano can be a fast, easy, profitable crop. Most experienced growers should be able to produce a nice crop of oregano plants in their first try.

October 1999

Success with Mints

Conrad Richter

If ever there were a cure for brown thumbs, mint would be it. The many mint varieties available are among the easiest of herbs to grow. Novice herb gardeners rarely have a problem growing them, and the enduring appeal of mints for tea and flavor in food make them an easy sell for spring pot production.

If there is a challenge for the commercial pot plant grower, it's finding the right propagative material to start with. Like other herbs that have long been misunderstood by the industry, starting with seeds is a recipe for disappointment. Although "peppermint" seeds are widely sold by seed companies, the true peppermint, *Mentha* x *piperita,* is a sterile hybrid that can't produce seeds. Artificial crossing of its putative parents is futile because any seeds produced by such crosses result in diverse forms, most of which won't possess the characteristic peppermint aroma and flavor. What is commonly sold as "peppermint" seed is in fact a rank-smelling form of spearmint (*Mentha spicata*), which has no value as a kitchen herb.

While commercial spearmint seeds are at least the correct species, plants grown from them have all the wrong combinations of essential oils, with, again, an undesirable level of odor and flavor.

Spearmint. *Photos by Richters Herbs.*

In all cases, the most desirable varieties of mint must be grown from cuttings or by root division. For commercial pot plant production, cuttings are the favored method. Dozens of varieties are available, but only a few are important for commercial horticulture. They include peppermint, spearmint, orange mint (*Mentha aquatica* 'Citrata'), ginger mint (*Mentha* x *gracilis* 'Variegata'), and two forms of spearmint, the improved spearmint, or Kentucky Colonel mint, and English mint. Orange mint is also known as bergamot mint or eau de cologne mint. As its names suggest, it has a sweet fruity or floral scent and flavor popular for tea and potpourri. Ginger mint isn't so notable for its mild, faintly reminiscent ginger flavor and aroma, but more for its attractive gold-flecked leaves. The improved spearmint and the English mint are both superior spearmint cultivars among hundreds of forms found in gardens. The improved form is more disease-resistant than the standard narrow-leafed variety, and the nearly round-leafed English variety has a milder, more refined aroma and flavor found in traditional mint jelly, peas, carrots, potatoes, mint julep, and lamb sauce.

Mint is most commonly grown and sold in 4-in. pots for spring sales. It's not suitable for pack sales because it grows root-bound quickly in cells. Mint is a quick crop from cuttings or liners, ready for sale in four to six weeks or less.

Ginger mint

Propagation

Liners are available from specialty herb plug growers. Cuttings are harder to find commercially, so most growers maintain their own stock plants. A single 5-gal. stock plant will produce dozens of cuttings a week; however, the cost of maintaining enough stock plants for sizable production cuts into potential profits.

Cuttings

Stem or root cuttings can be used, but stem cuttings are easier and quicker to handle. Cuttings 3 to 4 in. long are taken from clean stock plants. Soaking soft cuttings in water as they are being made keeps them turgid until ready to plant. Adding a contact miticide such as Safer's insecticidal soap to the soaking solution helps prevent pest infestation. Rooting hormone is optional, as mints root readily without it.

Rooting Medium

Lightweight peat-based rooting medium with 20% perlite added for drainage is ideal, but mint will root in any well-drained medium. The pH should be between 5 and 7. Watering trays before sticking cuttings ensures even moisture throughout.

Trays and Pots

A variety of 72 to 128 larger cell trays works well. Growers with sufficient space under mist can root cuttings directly in finished 3- to 4-in. pots.

Maintain 72 to 77°F during initial rooting phase. Keep humidity elevated between 90 to 100% under mist. Provide light shade from direct sun for the first two to three days until rooting begins. After seven to ten days, root development will be well under way and trays can be removed from misting bench. The temperature can be lowered to 64 to 72°F and humidity to 70 to 75%.

Fertilizing and Watering

When cuttings are removed from mist after seven to ten days, fertilize with one-third strength feeding at 35 to 50 ppm. Gradually increase to half strength, or 50 to 75 ppm, as plugs develop.

Growing On

Mint is a very quick crop that becomes saleable in 4-in. pots after only three to four weeks from plugs or four to six weeks when cuttings are stuck directly in 4-in. pots.

Rooted cuttings are ready for transplanting at three to four weeks when root balls are well developed but not to the point of being root-bound. Transplant the rooted cuttings in 4-in. pots.

Mint prefers a humus-rich soil mix with moisture retention ability and good drainage. Some growers prefer to use compost-based mixes with added peat and perlite.

Mints require a nighttime minimum temperature of 54°F and a daytime minimum of 61°F for active growth. A temperature above 86°F slows growth. Normal ambient greenhouse lighting and a humidity of 70% are adequate for mints.

Fertilization and Watering

Raise fertilizer level from half to full strength (100 to 150 ppm) with successive feedings. Keep the mint crop evenly moist because it won't tolerate drying out. Excessive drying out will cause the foliage to turn yellow.

Spacing and Pinching

After potting, plants can remain pot to pot up to four weeks, depending on variety and growth conditions. The central stem should be pinched back to encourage bushy growth. If plants become crowded, they must be pruned back or spaced. Stolons should be cut back to prevent plants from growing into each other. Ideally, plants should more or less fill the pot with foliage. There is a window of four weeks when mint plants must be moved out or they will become tangled and overgrown.

Pests and Diseases

Whitefly, spider mites, aphids, and thrips are the main mint crop pests. Because herbs are edible plants, there are few available controls when outbreaks of pests occur. Close monitoring of pest populations is the first and most important line of defense. Weekly examination of the crop with the aid of yellow and blue sticky traps will catch outbreaks at the earliest stages, when acceptable contact pesticides such as Safer's insecticidal soap are most effective. Other products suitable for application on edible plants introduced in the past five to ten years such as neem-based (e.g., Neemazad) and fungus-based (e.g., Naturalis-O) sprays are slower acting and may not provide effective control on fast crops like mint. Beneficials such as whitefly parasites and mite predators are not effective on fast growing crops.

Mint plants are susceptible to a rust for which there is no acceptable control, and symptoms (brown spots or patches on leaves) don't appear until midsummer. If rust appears on greenhouse plants, discard them and try a more resistant variety. For example, the standard spearmint is more susceptible than the improved spearmint or the English mint. Various wilting diseases are known to occur in production fields but are rarely seen in greenhouses.

Mint can be a fast and easy profitable crop, and growers should be able to produce a nice crop on their first try.

June 1999

Perennials: Surviving Freezing Temperatures

Researchers at Iowa State University subjected five perennial species to the ultimate test of cold hardiness, testing their ability to regrow after exposure to low temperatures. They froze fifteen of each plant at each temperature. Tests revealed that most species survived when exposed to 14°F, but damage increased as temperatures decreased. *Physostegia* was the most hardy, *Tanacetum* the least. Researchers advise growers producing perennials in containers to provide winter protection to prevent root media temperatures from falling below 14°F.

Effect of Low Temperatures on Percentage Survival of Perennials

Herbaceous perennial	Treatment Temperature (°F)									
	32	28	25	21	18	14	10	7	3	0
	Percentage of Test Plants Surviving									
'Goblin' *Gaillardia* x *grandiflora*	78	100	100	88	100	100	78	88	78	33
'Summer Snow' *Physostegia virginiana*	100	100	100	100	100	100	100	100	100	11
'Stratford Blue' *Salvia* x *superba*	100	100	88	88	100	100	67	78	67	11
'Robinson's Mix' *Tanacetum coccineum*	100	100	100	100	88	88	44	0	0	0
Veronica repens	100	100	100	100	100	100	78	22	22	0

January 1997

Chapter 2
Propagation

Techniques for Winter Propagation

Martha Simon Pindale

The key to winter propagation is to be creative and plan ahead. There is so much to do in the spring that it's helpful to cross as much off the propagation list as possible during the winter. Here are some tips for propagating by division or root cuttings. Also included is a list of the plants we propagated during the winter at Bluemount Nurseries Inc.

Division

When it comes to division, the sky is the limit. Keep track of where you place various species so you can easily find them for propagation during the winter.

Remove the plants from the pots to observe the roots. Are they going around the pot, or are they barely visible? Can you make more plants out of them, or should you keep the plant to sell next year? Perhaps you could steal some of the small shoots that are growing around the edge of the pot and keep the original plant for sale.

For example, *Achillea millefolium* can be removed from the pot and many of the small runners removed. The large plant can be saved for sale for the next year. *Aegopodium* can be handled in the same way. Small runners can be pulled off and potted, saving the original plant. This technique also works with *Armeria maritima, Aster, Astilbe,* and *Coreopsis verticillata* 'Moonbeam'. With 'Moonbeam', which can be a finicky plant, remove the plant from a quart pot, collect little side shoots that have formed, and put them in the plug trays. In February when they start growing, you can take more cuttings.

When you chop a plant, put the cuttings into plugs or 1-qt. pots, depending on the plant. We place them in a cold tunnel, preferably with double fleece. A minimal heat house would be the best, but they're expensive, and there isn't always room.

Something to remember with winter divisions is that you need to leave some of the originals for early sales. Customers aren't going to be too happy if everything is in 1-qt. containers. Simply leave ⅓ or ½ for early sales, and propagate them later in the season if needed.

Watering

Remember to water plants well before placing them in the houses. We usually don't water during winter unless it's absolutely necessary. Occasionally, we go through the houses and check the water conditions. New cuttings or divisions don't use a lot of water, so they don't need much water. Workers need to be trained that it's OK if the top inch is dry. The roots are further down, and the plant isn't using much water. When we go through the houses, if there is a species or even individual pots that need water, we gently water just the top. This is another area where you'll need to watch your employees. They'll often have a hard time watering just the top of the pots, so you'll need to train them in this area well.

Temperatures

The temperature of the house should be around 32°F. Freezing is OK, but you can't let the house get down to 22°F for extended periods of time. If you're in a region where temperatures are low for a long period of time, you'll have to take more precautions. Always err on the side of caution. Ice is a great insulator, but it can be a pain to handle. Try a polyhouse and fleece blankets.

Root Cuttings

Root cuttings are great for the winter months, though they do take up a lot space. For example, five thousand *Geranium sanguineum* plugs require a lot of bench space. Ideally, they should have bottom heat (about 75°F) twenty-four hours per day.

Something else to keep in mind is where you're going to get this material. You need a good, thick root, at least the

By propagating perennials such as *Coreopsis* 'Moonbeam' during the winter, you'll have beautiful flowering plants for spring sales.

size of a pencil. You can propagate from some of the plants in your display gardens, from containers, and from field plants.

You can also buy stock plants from other growers, but there is a drawback to this, and it is that you don't know what you're going to get until you open the box. Try to multi-source every year. Depending on the species, try to get about two thousand root cuttings so you have something for summer potting for next year.

Another problem with getting plants from other sources is that you have to watch for pests. For example, in Maryland, root knot nematode is a big problem for farmers, and inspectors watch very closely for this particular pest. Also a potential problem is an awful weed called keik, which is in the mustard family. It has very fine roots that intertwine readily. It is low-growing, compact, and has numerous seeds. It also readily propagates from root cuttings. If you find any in a pot, throw out the entire pot. No chemicals or herbicides will control this plant, and if you leave even a fraction of the root, it will come back.

Polarity

You should also consider polarity, the orientation of the root cutting. What was up must remain up, and what was down must still face down. For some species, it is very important; for others, it doesn't matter at all. Some species where polarity is important are: *Acanthus, Papaver, Anchusa,* and *Asclepias.*

A good rule of thumb is that the bigger and thicker the root, the more orientation matters. Pick the roots that are the thickest. Thin isn't good when it comes to root cuttings, and you also need to decide what to do with the mother plant. Are you going to take every last root possible, or are you going to try to save the plant and take three to four roots off every mother plant? For example, one nice thing about *Acanthus* is that the more you dig, the more small plants you get. Simply dig one main plant; then dig the little ones and pot them.

A good way to identify polarity is to make an angled cut at the bottom and a straight cut at the top. This way you can tell at a glance which way is up when the roots are in a pile. Hold as many roots as you can, and make one cut instead of cutting roots individually. The pieces should be 1½ to 2 in. long.

Stick the root cuttings into a 70 tray vertically and water them well. Once they've been watered, keep them as dry as possible. It will take weeks to form new roots, so they don't need much water. Don't leave anything sticking out. If you do, just cover it with a light layer.

Fungicides aren't necessary if you're digging a healthy crop from the field, your mix is sterile, and the tools are clean.

Winter-Propagated Species at Bluemount Nurseries Inc.

Division	Root cuttings	Seed frost germinators	Seed spring bloomers	Grasses	Potting bulbs
Achillea	Acanthus	Alchemilla	Adenophora	Arundo donax	Anemone
Aegopodium	Anemone	Amsonia	Aethionema	Calamagrostis	blanda
'America'	Anchusa	Aruncus	Alcea	Deschampsia	Allium
Aster	Asclepias	Gentiana	Anthemis	Festuca	caeruleum
Astilbe	Brunnera	Helleborus	Aquilegia	Glyceria	A. moly
Boltonia	Dicentra	Lobelia	Arabis	Helicotrichon	A. oreophilum
Chrysanthemum	spectabilis	Primula	Armeria	Miscanthus	Arum italicum
Coreopsis	Geranium	Rudbeckia	Aubrieta	Molinia	'Pictum'
'Moonbeam'	sanguineum	'Goldsturm'	Aurinia	Panicum	Lily
Coreopsis rosea	Paeonia	Tricyrtis	Bellis	Pennisetum	Oxalis
Epimedium	Papaver		Campanula	Phalaris	adenophylla
Filipendula	Phlox		Cerastium	Saccharum	
Helianthus	paniculata		Coreopsis	Erianthus	
Helenium	Stokesia		Delphinium		
Hemerocallis			Dianthus		
Hosta			Digitalis		
Houttuynia			Doronicum		
Liriope			Geum		
Lysimachia			Linum		
Monarda			Lupinus		
Physostegia			Myosotis		
Rudbeckia			Papaver		
Sedum			Polemonium		
Sempervivum			Saponaria		
Solidago			Viola		
Stokesia					
Tradescantia					
Vernonia					

October 1998

Perennial Plugs—The Sensible Solution

Paul and Paula Yantorno

Want to grow more perennials, faster and cheaper? Plugs may be the answer!

With specialization a key to survival, plug production can be one less specialty that growers need to worry about. And annual plugs aren't your only plug option. Buying in perennial plugs can make sense for growers who are looking at the expense, the time, and the space required to produce a quality perennial crop from start to finish. With top producers throughout the U.S. selling high-quality, ready-to-finish perennial plugs, there's no shortage of supply if you decide not to seed your own.

Benefits of Plugs

Perennial seed germination can be very erratic. Starting a crop with plugs that are actively growing is one way to accurately predict a finished crop. For growers unfamiliar with perennial varieties, the guesswork has been taken out of what to grow. Many producers have regional collections or suggestions to fit into any marketing program. Variety lists that focus on the best and most important perennials have been identified and heavily researched.

Many growers who take into account the amount of space and handling required to get a crop to the plug stage will opt to let the plug producer do his part. Because many perennial varieties require a cold treatment before flowering, purchasing vernalized plugs saves time and money. One of the benefits of using vernalized plugs is having flowering perennial plants to sell the first year. Starting a perennial crop from plugs ensures a fast takeoff and quick turns from valuable greenhouse space. Finish time can be as short as six weeks for some varieties!

Liners are shipped ready to plant. The plug supplier has the responsibility of maintaining the inventory, and with accurate scheduling, the grower can have multiple ship dates and fresh perennial plugs to plant.

Perennial Plug Culture

Perennials are available in several plug sizes, such as 128-count (sold as 125s). Their finish time is slightly longer than 72-count (sold as 70s). These larger plugs are best when a quicker finish is required. They're good for a fast, 4-in. finished pot size and for wintering over. Plant one to three plugs per 1-gal. container, depending on the variety and the plug size. For example, 'Blue Emerald' *Phlox subulata* requires three plugs (either 125-count or 70-count size) per gallon, while one plug is recommended for 'Allegro' *Papaver orientale*.

A soilless mix with good drainage and water retention is best for planting perennials. Perennials tend to be heavier feeders than foliage plants and trees or shrubs. Nutrition level recommendations include:

- pH: 6.6 to 6.8
- Ammonia nitrogen: 50 to 150 ppm
- Nitrate nitrogen: 350 to 800 ppm
- Phosphate phosphorus: 125 to 350 ppm
- Potassium (potash): 350 to 800 ppm
- Calcium: 1,000 to 4,000 ppm
- Specific conductance: 1550 to 225 micromhos

Perennial plugs shouldn't be held too long before planting. Keep them cool (45°F) and in bright light. Like annual plugs, perennial liners are moisture sensitive, so keep them from drying out.

Once planted, greenhouse temperatures (55 to 60°F nights and 60 to 65°F days) and the fertilizer regimen should be adjusted to promote root growth while keeping shoot/crown growth as compact as possible. High light levels and night lighting (400+ f.c.) is also helpful in assuring good growth and compactness under winter's normally low-light conditions. As soon as the plant is well-rooted (four to six weeks) and the crown is well-developed, greenhouse temperatures should be lowered to 35 to 40°F (day and night) for ten weeks for hardening and vernalization.

Vernalization

Generally, 70-count and 125-count plugs, purchased non-vernalized, can be planted in 1-gal pots in January, after Christmas crops have shipped. Hardened off from February 15 through March 1 at 32°F, they can then be vernalized outside (freeing up greenhouse space for bedding annuals) from March 1 through shipping. Plant 70-count plugs in 4-in. pots during week two or three; harden off at 32°F from February 15 through March 1; vernalize outside from March 1 through shipping. If outside temperatures are going to be below 30°F, newly planted plugs should be covered at night or grown inside for at least two weeks or until rooted. After two weeks, perennial plugs can handle cooler temperatures.

Michigan State University research has found that juvenility is one factor in successful vernalization. Cold treatment is effective only if the plug is old enough. Plug size doesn't always mean older plugs. Although it differs by variety, ten to sixteen leaf pairs seem to be enough for the vernalization process. Good plug producers use this as a measure of readiness.

Some perennial varieties than benefit from vernalization, such as *Lavandula angustifolia* and *Liatris spicata,* can be purchased pre-vernalized, which can cut your finishing time. Many perennials—especially mid-summer- through fall-blooming varieties and many groundcovers—don't require vernalization, so they can be scheduled for later planting, similar to other flowering crops. Growing on at cold temperatures is beneficial for producing a high-quality finished perennial, both inside and outside the greenhouse.

Fall Sales and Overwintering

Summer- or fall-planted perennial crops can be used for fall sales and to winter over. Production can be handled exclusively outdoors, or inside the greenhouse, depending on the type of facility available, the climate, and the size liner purchased. Slower-growing varieties that rely on underground buds or roots for survival, and 125-count plugs, should be planted in late July or early August to allow adequate rooting and bud development before the onset of severe weather. Faster-growing varieties in 125-count and 70-count plugs can be planted during August or September, depending on species. Keep fertility on the higher end of recommended ammonium nitrogen rates and moderate nitrate nitrogen rates initially to promote stem growth, branching, and bud set. To help harden stem growth and promote root development, decrease the ammonium nitrogen as the fall season progresses.

A bushy, well-rooted plant with a well-developed crown will survive the next steps of drying down and mild stressing, necessary to further the hardening process. Once the plants appear dormant and soil in the container is frozen, provide winter protection. Prior to covering with a frost cloth, check for excessive moisture and use a cover spray of fungicide to prevent crown rot and foliar diseases. Winter watering is necessary in cold, dry climates like Colorado.

Uncover perennials promptly in the spring to prevent stretching. A spring fertilizing plan with moderate levels of nitrate nitrogen will assure a harder perennial with a healthy flush of spring growth.

Pest Control

Perennials are susceptible to many of the same insect and disease problems as other plants. Good perennial plug suppliers will have screened stock and propagation areas and will ship only clean cuttings. Watering early in the day and as infrequently as possible, combined with proper pot spacing and good ventilation, will reduce the chance for disease contamination. Using a fertilizer high in nitrate nitrogen rather than ammonia nitrogen will also help produce a healthy perennial crop.

The control of powdery mildew, *Botrytis,* and rusts are a special concern in winter and early spring. Preventative measures such as sulfur burners and fungicide cover sprays are essential to successfully grow perennials such as *Veronica, Verbena,* and *Monarda.*

Monitoring insects with sticky traps, then applying pesticides or biological controls as needed, will help prevent serious insect infestations. Thrips carry tomato spotted wilt virus and impatiens necrotic spot virus, which are easily spread and symptomatic only at high (over 70 to 75°F) temperatures. Perennials are asymptomatic—they don't show symptoms of these viruses, but they can be carriers. Purchasing liners from a reputable supplier ensures clean plants. Prevent foliar diseases with fungicide cover sprays such as Cleary's, Phyton, Subdue, and Benomyl. Consult your local extension office for assistance and specific pest problems.

Why Do It All

Perennial plug producers have a lot to offer. They can help you focus on your specific area of expertise—that of providing a top-quality finished plant. Buying in perennial plugs can save time, money, and valuable greenhouse production space. Purchasing perennial plugs is the sensible answer for the finish grower who asks the question, "Should I try to do it all?"

February 1997

Bluemount Nursery on Propagating Grasses

We dig grasses between Thanksgiving and Christmas, shake off as much of the soil as we can, place them into a cold tunnel, and put a woven wool thermal blanket over them. During the winter, we can obtain the grasses, one species at a time, from the tunnel to use for propagation.

Keep in mind that the younger the grass stock is, the better it propagates. The older the clump, the harder it is to propagate. A one- or two-year-old clump is the best.

As far as tools go, you can use whatever you have available, a hatchet, pitchfork, chainsaw, or whatever works best for you.

We do the divisions, pot them, and place them in the minimum heat house (33 to 35°F). We keep the house as dry as possible. Grasses don't like water in the winter; they aren't putting on any new growth, so why water them?

If you're short on space, you can pack the grasses into boxes; then put them into the cooler. In May, pot them up, and they'll be salable by July. Line the bottoms of the boxes with plastic and some moist peat moss so they don't get too wet. Note: The one major drawback to this method is that it's easy to forget the boxes sitting in your cooler, especially when you're so busy potting everything else.

One grass species that doesn't like this method is *Pennisetum.* Try to leave it in the ground as late as possible and store it for as little time as possible. The longer it's stored, the less success you'll have. *Pennisetum orientale* is only produced in containers. We seed into plugs and plant those right into 1-gal. containers for sale.

With some of the evergreen-type grasses, you can leave several containers for production. Late in the season, divide them and put them into plugs. When they start to grow, you can even divide them again and get more plugs.

For *Calamagrostis,* put it into a 32-plug tray. Don't be stingy with the divisions. Don't put little divisions into the gallons; they won't fill out. They'll look small all summer and they won't sell. Make bigger divisions so they look nice and fill the container.

As far as container size goes, it's hard to say what is the best. You can put the runner types of species into bigger containers and literally watch them fill in, but with some of the others, you have to use small containers. It depends on the species and what you want the plant to look like when the customer first sees it.

October 1998

Chapter 3
Height Control and PGRs

Manipulating Photoperiod for Height Control

Paul Koreman, Art Cameron, Royal Heins, and Will Carlson

Limited induction photoperiod is a non-chemical technique for controlling elongation of long-day herbaceous perennials. It allows growers to control the height of long-day plants by simply manipulating the photoperiod.

Two plant responses to long days help explain how limited induction photoperiod works: First, some long-day plants respond to long days by bolting. Second, many long-day plant species require only a limited number of long-day cycles to induce flower bud formation. Long days increase the production and sensitivity of some plants to gibberellic acid, a hormone that promotes stem elongation. As long as these plants perceive long days, they'll continue to produce gibberellic acid and elongate. Under short-day conditions, the gibberellic acid production decreases dramatically, and elongation, or bolting, stops. When flower buds begin to form, their continued development doesn't require continuous long days. For plants that are responsive to limited induction photoperiod, the length of the photoperiod after flower induction won't affect whether the plant will flower.

Researchers at the University of Virginia, Blacksburg, successfully used limited induction photoperiod on *Coreopsis* 'Early Sunrise', using sixteen long days followed by short days. At Michigan State University, we continued that research with great success, producing plants that were shorter at first flower, although there was some delay in bloom time and reduction in flower number. Limited induction photoperiod was effective on 'Early Sunrise' and six other plants tests; the exception was *Coreopsis* 'Baby Sun'. In this limited induction photoperiod screen, plants were grown under long days for two, three, four, or five weeks before transfer back to nineteen-hour days for finishing. *Coreopsis* 'Baby Sun' and 'Sunray' plants given limited induction photoperiod treatment didn't have as many buds at first flower as continuously lit controls. Below a critical number, fewer long days resulted in shorter plants but also delayed bloom.

In another experiment, 'Early Sunrise' plants were given sixteen long days and then grown to flower under eight day lengths ranging from nine to twenty-four

Coreopsis lanceolata 'Early Sunrise' plants were given a limited number of long days, then finished under nine-hour photoperiods. Shorter-blooming plants were the result of this treatment.

hours of light. As the daylength after limited induction photoperiod treatment increased, plant height increased. Plants finished under photoperiods of fourteen hours or fewer had no delay in bloom but a significant reduction in height. The most horticulturally acceptable plants were finished under the twelve-hour photoperiods.

Limited induction photoperiod on perennial species

	Days of limited induction photoperiod	Reduce height	Delay bloom	Decrease flower number	Flowering percentage
Campanula carpatica 'Blue Clips'	21	Yes	No	Yes	90
Coreopsis grandiflora 'Sunburst'	28	Yes	No	Yes	40
Coreopsis grandiflora 'Sunray'	21	Yes	No	No	100
Coreopsis lanceolata 'Baby Sun'	28	No	No	No	20
Coreopsis lanceolata 'Early Sunrise'	21	Yes	Yes	Yes	100
Coreopsis verticillata 'Moonbeam'	14	Yes	No	Yes	100
Echinacea purpurea	28	Yes	No	Yes	50

In this experiment, plants were given fourteen, twenty-one, twenty-eight, or thirty-five days of night interruption. Next, they were finished under a nine-hour day length. Limited induction photoperiod reduced height on all but one of the species tested. Flowering percentage in limited induction photoperiod treatments wasn't significantly different than controls exposed to continuous night interruption.

It's possible to tell when *Coreopsis* is being grown under long days by observing the leaf orientation, because leaves turn upright after two or three long days following transfer from short days. Leaves on plants under short days remain horizontal. However, three days aren't enough to induce 100% flowering. For the 'Early Sunrise' we tested, twenty-one long days were needed to achieve 100% flowering.

The height reduction appears to be effective only on internodes on the vegetative portion of the plant. Therefore, if you give plants long days until visible bud, there may be no reduction in height from limited induction photoperiod because internodes will already have elongated.

Limited induction photoperiod can be used on *Coreopsis* 'Early Sunrise' without black cloth when the natural day length is shorter than fourteen hours. 'Early Sunrise' blooms in about sixty days at 68°F with supplemental high-pressure sodium lights. If a northern grower wants to have 'Early Sunrise' in flower on May 1, the long-day treatment should start on March 1, and

Echinacea purpurea plants were given zero, two, three, four, and five weeks of long days as four-hour night interruption, then transferred back to nine-hour photoperiods. The photo was taken eight weeks after the first exposure to long days.

the lights should be turned off on March 21. The natural day length at this time is around twelve hours, so black cloth shouldn't be needed right away. Using three weeks of long days instead of sixteen days ensures that 100% of the plants are induced, according to our results. When the natural day length extends beyond fourteen hours in early May, 'Early Sunrise' plants will resume bolting unless black cloth is used to maintain a short photoperiod. If photoperiod control isn't available, growth regulators may be required at the end of the production cycle.

Growers already equipped with chrysanthemum lighting can use limited induction photoperiod during the winter and early spring with no changes to their existing setup. Further research will refine the technology, but limited induction photoperiod appears to be a viable, non-chemical method of height control for some long-day plants.

Editor's note: The authors would like to thank industry supporters who made research for this article possible, as well as thank Cheryl Hamaker, Cara Wallace and Tom Wallace.

December 1996

Combining PGRs Yields Better Results

Paul Pilon

How many times have you been dissatisfied with the amount of control you received from a plant growth regulator application? Are there some specific varieties you wish you could find a height control solution for? If you found a good control strategy, could you sell more plants?

With the ever-increasing introduction and popularity of new plant varieties of both perennials and vegetative annuals, we growers are facing many new challenges. Besides managing the many cultural aspects of producing these modern crops, we have to produce plants that have very specific characteristics, such as shape and size.

Researchers aren't keeping up with the growth control needs of many of the new plant species, either. And often, breeder or distributor recommendations aren't adequate to meet our commercial needs. At Sawyer Nursery in Hudsonville, Michigan, where I'm head grower, I've found that A-Rest, used in combination with other plant growth regulators, may provide the synergy needed to achieve adequate height control of some of these tough-to-control varieties.

Getting Technical

All of the commercially available plant growth regulators essentially control plant height by interfering with the biosynthesis of gibberellins within the plant. Gibberellin promotes cell elongation, which in turn contributes to the plant's overall height. Each plant growth regulator interferes with the biosynthesis process at a different site. Thus, quite often when two different growth regulators are combined, there's a greater response than when a chemical is used alone. This heightened response to the combination is referred to as synergy. The level of synergy observed is dependent on many factors, such as the chemicals being combined, the rates of each chemical used, the plant they're being applied to, and the age or stage of development of the plant.

In-House Research

At Sawyer Nursery, we've improved many aspects of crop production using growth regulators. For perennials, A-Rest, B-Nine, and Sumagic all provide good response across a wide range of plant varieties. Improvements include increased uniformity, improved plant color, higher plant quality, a longer shelf life, and less shrink (meaning more salable plants!).

However, for many species, growth regulators haven't provided us with enough control when used alone. Therefore, we began conducting our own research, using these growth regulators individually and in various combinations, to find the best PGRs for the varieties that have been difficult for us to control. Our goals were to gain some synergy from combining two chemicals, obtain greater control of plant height in difficult to control varieties, and use A-Rest in a more cost-effective manner. With many of the varieties tested, we observed impressive results. In some cases, plant height was reduced by as much as 37% using an A-Rest/B-Nine tank mixture.

We conducted trials on several perennial varieties grown in quart pots at a pot-tight spacing, which is typical of commercial perennial production. Each treatment was applied three times, at one-week intervals. Evaluations were conducted each week to determine the plant response to the applications.

We got excellent results using A-Rest plus B-Nine on *Boltonia* 'Pink Beauty'. Three applications of A-Rest at 25 ppm reduced overall plant height by only 3%. Three applications of B-Nine at 2,500 ppm decreased plant height by 23%. However, three applications of the tank mixture of A-Rest at 15 ppm plus B-Nine at 1,250 ppm reduced overall plant height by an impressive 37%. Note that the total cumulative ppm of each A-Rest and B-Nine was half (or nearly half), when used in the tank mixture compared with each chemical applied alone.

We got similar excellent results when applying a tank mixture of A-Rest plus B-Nine to *Aquilegia* 'Star Series'. When three applications of A-rest at 25 ppm were applied, the plant height was reduced by 8%. B-Nine applied three times at 2,500 ppm reduced plant height by 18%. The synergetic combination of A-Rest at 15 ppm plus B-Nine at 1,250 ppm (again, about half the rate of each) reduced plant height by an astounding 35% when applied three times.

There seemed to be less synergy when combining A-Rest with Sumagic than with the A-Rest/B-Nine combinations. This may mean that these chemicals reduce the biosynthesis of gibberellins at similar sites, which wouldn't yield as much synergy. Quite often the reduction in plant height using an A-Rest plus Sumagic was similar to using Sumagic alone. For instance, three applications of A-Rest at 25 ppm reduced plant height by 8%. Sumagic at 5 ppm applied three times reduced the height by 17%, and the tank mixture of A-Rest at 15 ppm plus Sumagic at 2.5 ppm reduced plant height by only 19% when applied three times.

However, some plant varieties did display some synergy to the A-Rest plus Sumagic mix. With *Gaillardia* 'Burgundy', A-Rest at 25 ppm applied three times reduced the plant height by 14%. Three applications of Sumagic at 5 ppm reduced the height by 21%. And the combination of A-Rest at 15 ppm plus Sumagic at 2.5 ppm reduced the overall plant height by 27%.

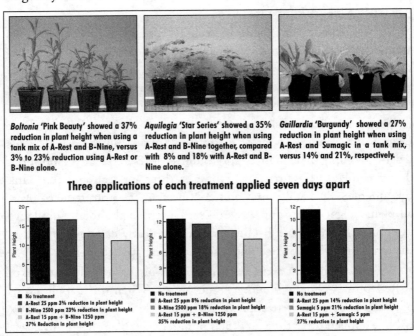

Boltonia 'Pink Beauty' showed a 37% reduction in plant height when using a tank mix of A-Rest and B-Nine, versus 3% to 23% reduction using A-Rest or B-Nine alone.

Aquilegia 'Star Series' showed a 35% reduction in plant height when using A-Rest and B-Nine together, compared with 8% and 18% with A-Rest and B-Nine alone.

Gaillardia 'Burgundy' showed a 27% reduction in plant height when using A-Rest and Sumagic in a tank mix, versus 14% and 21%, respectively.

Three applications of each treatment applied seven days apart

- ■ No treatment
- ■ A-Rest 25 ppm 3% reduction in plant height
- ▨ B-Nine 2500 ppm 23% reduction in plant height
- ▨ A-Rest 15 ppm + B-Nine 1250 ppm 37% Reduction in plant height

- ■ No treatment
- ■ A-Rest 25 ppm 8% reduction in plant height
- ▨ B-Nine 2500 ppm 18% reduction in plant height
- ▨ A-Rest 15 ppm + B-Nine 1250 ppm 35% reduction in plant height

- ■ No treatment
- ■ A-Rest 25 ppm 14% reduction in plant height
- ▨ Sumagic 5 ppm 21% reduction in plant height
- ▨ A-Rest 15 ppm + Sumagic 5 ppm 27% reduction in plant height

Cost and Recommendations

One concern of growers when using A-Rest has been its high cost relative to other PGRs. When using A-Rest tank mixtures only for niche applications or on difficult-to-control varieties, these synergetic combinations may be more expensive than traditional growth regulator applications on a per-square-foot basis, but the costs are quite insignificant when amortized over all of the crops being produced. Most growers would rather have high-quality salable plants as opposed to lanky, low-quality plants that won't be purchased, even if it costs slightly more to produce them.

For growers who produce perennials or new species of vegetative annuals, I'd first recommend trying Sumagic. In Michigan, I find two or three applications of Sumagic at 5 ppm roughly seven days apart to be very effective on most species. B-Nine is also very effective on a wide array of plant species. Typically, I've found that 2,500 ppm applied two or three times yields good results.

If you don't get adequate control with Sumagic, B-Nine, or another plant growth regulator, consider tank mixing them with A-Rest. If I had to suggest one combination for these niche applications, it would be A-Rest at 10 ppm plus B-Nine at 1,250 ppm. Try using this on a small scale to determine its effectiveness before making any major applications.

Remember: No one growth regulator will control plant height on all plant varieties, and similarly, no single combination of these chemicals is likely to yield comparable results on all species of plants. And don't make drastic changes to your current growth control strategies. Run some tests as we did, and check the results for yourself.

June 2001

Using Growth Regulators to Control Height of Herbaceous Perennials

Cheryl K. Hamaker, Beth E. Engle, Royal D. Heins, William H. Carlson, and Arthur C. Cameron

Anyone familiar with flowering herbaceous perennials knows they include a range of species that grow very tall, especially when forced in a greenhouse. Shorter species also may develop flowers on extremely tall spikes. When in flower, these plants can be very difficult to ship and display. Retailers find that a good-looking perennial plant in flower sells; customers prefer a plant in bloom for the immediate show that its flowers provide in the garden. However, even when in flower, a tall or floppy plant is not as appealing.

Figure 1. *Gaura lindheimeri* 'Whirling Butterflies' was unresponsive to all chemical growth regulators.

As part of ongoing research in perennials at Michigan State University, we have screened growth regulators to determine their effectiveness on a variety of herbaceous perennials. The objective has been to determine whether a growth regulator was effective on a particular species, not to determine recommended rates for that species.

While all five of the common growth regulators used in the floricultural industry,

Table 1. Species where flowering was delayed by five or more days by applications of 5,000 ppm B-Nine every ten days when compared to untreated plants.

Scientific Name	Common Name
Achillea millefolium 'Summer Pastels'	Common yarrow
Alcea rosea 'Chater's Double Mix'	Hollyhock
Aster alpinus 'Alpine Mix'	Alpine aster
Campanula carpatica 'Blue Clips'	Carpathian harebell
Chrysanthemum coccineum 'J. Kelway'	Painted daisy
Coreopsis grandiflora 'Sunray'	Tickseed
Coreopsis verticillata 'Moonbeam'	Threadleaf coreopsis
Heuchera sanguinea 'Bressingham'	Coral bells
Lavandula angustifolia 'Munstead Dwarf'	Lavender
Lobelia x *hybrida* 'Queen Victoria'	Cardinal flower
Lobelia x *speciosa* 'Compliment Scarlet'	Sweet lobelia
Perovskia atriplicifolia	Russian sage
Salvia x *superba* 'Blue Queen'	Sage

ancydimol (A-Rest), daminozide (B-Nine), paclobutrazol (Bonzi), chlormequat (Cycocel), and uniconazole (Sumagic), reduce stem elongation of some floricultural crops, none reduces stem elongation of all species and little is known about their effectiveness on perennials. How will they work on perennials?

The five growth regulators we tested as spray applications were 100 ppm A-Rest, 5,000 ppm B-Nine, 30 ppm Bonzi, 1,500 ppm Cycocel, and 15 ppm Sumagic. The rates used during testing were high to assure plant response; they are not necessarily recommended for commercial height-control programs.

During the last three years, we've been able to determine growth response of thirty-five species to these five chemicals. Field-grown divisions or fifty-cell plugs were planted into 1-gal. containers or 4- or 5-in. pots, respectively. All plants were grown at 68°F under a four-hour night interruption delivered from 10 P.M. to 2 A.M. by high-pressure sodium lamps. Transplants were given time for establishment and then were sprayed with the growth regulators at ten-day intervals until flower. We measured height every ten days. Time to visible bud and flower, number of inflorescences, and final plant height were recorded for each treatment. We treated ten plants with each growth regulator and compared them to untreated plants. If there was no discernable difference in height between treated and untreated plants after at least three applications, we concluded that the growth regulator was not effective in controlling that species' stem elongation.

Plant response varied among growth regulators (table 2). A single growth regulator did not effectively control the height of every species, although most species responded to at least one chemical. B-Nine and Sumagic were the most effective growth regulators tested, reducing the height of twenty-three and twenty-four species respectively. A-Rest, Bonzi, and Cycocel were effective on twenty, twenty-one, and thirteen species respectively.

Seven species responded in some degree to all growth regulators. Unfortunately, four of the taller species, *Chelone glabra, Gaillardia* x *grandiflora, Gaura lindheimeri* (figure 1) and *Physostegia virginiana*, were unresponsive to any spray treatments. Higher rates than those we used may be necessary to control the height of these species. The timing of a growth regulator application is critical on species that bolt or have

Table 2. The relative effectiveness of repeated applications of 100 ppm ancydimol (A-Rest), 5,000 ppm daminozide (B-Nine), 30 ppm paclobutrazol (Bonzi), 1,500 ppm chlormequat (Cycocel). or 15 ppm uniconazole (Sumagic) on 35 species of herbaceous perennials. The rates tested were high to determine qualitative plant response and are not necessarily recommended for use in commercial industry.

Herbaceous Perennial Response to Growth Regulators

Species		Growth Regulators				
Scientific Name	Common Name	A-Rest	B-Nine	Bonzi	Cycocel	Sumagic
Achillea millefolium 'Summer Pastels'	Common yarrow	moderate	no	slight	no	strong
Alcea rosea 'Chater's Double Mix'	Hollyhock	slight	no	no	moderate	moderate
Asclepias tuberosa	Butterfly weed	no	no	strong	no	moderate
Aster alpinus 'Alpine Mix'	Alpine aster	no	no	no	no	strong
Astilbe x arendsii 'Bressingham Beauty'	Astilbe	moderate	no	slight	no	no
Campanula carpatica 'Blue Clips'	Carpathian harebell	strong	strong	strong	strong	strong
Campanula persicifolia 'Blue'	Bellflower	no	no	no	no	strong
Centaurea montana 'Violet'	Mountain bluet	no	no	no	no	strong
Chelone glabra	Turtlehead	no	no	no	no	no
Chrysanthemum coccineum 'J. Kelway'	Painted daisy	moderate	no	slight	strong	slight
Coreopsis grandiflora 'Sunray'	Tickseed	moderate	no	no	no	slight
Coreopsis verticillata 'Moonbeam'	Threadleaf coreopsis	no	no	no	no	no
Delphinium elatum 'Mix'	Delphinium	no	no	no	no	no
Echinacea purpurea 'Bravado'	Purple coneflower	moderate	no	no	strong	no
Gaillardia x grandiflora 'Burgundy'	Blanket flower	no	no	no	no	no
Gaura lindheimeri 'Whirling Butterflies'	Gaura	no	no	no	slight	no
Gypsophila paniculata 'Double Snowflake'	Baby's-breath	no	no	no	no	no
Helenium autumnale	Sneezeweed	no	moderate	no	no	no
Hemerocallis 'Hall's Pink'	Daylily	strong	no	no	no	no
Heuchera sanguinea 'Bressingham'	Coral bells	no	no	no	no	no
Hibiscus x hybrida 'Disco Belle Mix'	Mallow	no	no	no	no	strong
Lavandula angustifolia 'Munstead Dwarf'	Lavender	moderate	no	slight	no	no
Leucanthemum x superbum 'Marconi'	Shasta daisy	no	no	strong	no	moderate
Linum perenne 'Sapphire'	Flax	slight	no	no	no	no
Lobelia x hybrida 'Queen Victoria'	Cardinal flower	no	no	no	no	no
Lobelia x speciosa 'Compliment Scarlet'	Sweet lobelia	no	no	no	no	no
Perovskia atriplicifolia	Russian sage	no	no	no	no	no
Phlox paniculata 'Eva Cullum'	Summer phlox	no	no	no	no	no
Physostegia virginiana 'Summer Snow'	Obedient plant	no	no	no	no	no
Rudbeckia fulgida 'Goldsturm'	Black-eyed Susan	no	no	no	no	no
Salvia x superba 'Blue Queen'	Sage	slight	no	no	no	no
Sedum spurium 'Dragon's Blood'	Sedum	no	no	no	no	no
Veronica longifolia 'Red Fox'	Speedwell	strong	no	slight	no	no
Veronica longifolia 'Sunny Border Blue'	Speedwell	strong	strong	moderate	no	no
Veronica spicata 'Blue'	Speedwell	moderate	no	no	no	no

☐ no response   ▨ slight response   ▨ moderate response   ■ strong response

extremely fast developmental rates from visible bud to flower, such as *Aster alpinus*, *Astilbe* x *arendsii* (figure 2), and *Echinacea purpurea*. For these species, the growth regulator must be applied just at or just before the rapid elongation phase of development.

Figure 2. *Astilbe* x *arendsii* 'Bressingham Beauty' was only slightly responsive to growth regulators probably because the sequence of applications missed the rapid elongation phase.

Another factor to consider is the degree to which some species growth must be retarded. Rates used in this trial were designed to determine efficacy, and applications at the experimental rates may result in excessive height control. For example, *Campanula carpatica* 'Blue Clips' (figure 3) was severely stunted. However, it is possible to reduce the final height of a species slightly using growth regulators at lower rates.

Figure 3. Species such as *Campanula carpatica* 'Blue Clips' responded dramatically to chemical growth regulators. The excessive response of *C. carpatica* can be prevented through lower application rates or fewer applications.

Also included in the evaluation of responsiveness to different growth regulators were timing of bloom, flower number, and physiological disorders caused by sensitivity to a specific growth regulator. In our experience, treating with 5,000 ppm B-Nine occasionally caused a flowering delay (table 1), such as those of *Achillea millefolium* and *Coreopsis verticillata* (figure 4). As is well documented on other species, Cycocel causes foliar chlorosis on a number of herbaceous perennials. Species with the most severe chlorosis were *Chelone glabra* and *Hibiscus* x *hybrida*.

Figure 4. Growth regulators occasionally cause flowering delay. Applications of 5,000 ppm B-Nine effectively reduced height of *Coreopsis verticillata* 'Moonbeam', but delayed flowering compared to other treatments.

The use of growth regulators to control the height of larger, unruly species may be an effective strategy to increase their attractiveness. Specific application rates are difficult to recommend because of differences in climate, greenhouse, species, pot size, growing technique, and final desired height. If you do test any of these growth regulators, we suggest initial applications be made at 50 ppm R-Rest, 2,500 ppm B-Nine, 15 ppm Bonzi, 1,500 ppm Cycocel, or 10 ppm Sumagic. If height is shorter or taller than desired, adjust application frequency and rates based on your experience.

Editor's note: The authors would like to thank generous industry supporters who made possible the research this article was based on, as well as Shannon Strauch, Cara Wallace, Tom Wallace, and Kate Wanagat.

September 1996

Perennial Production: PGR Solutions for Your Greenhouse

Paul Pilon

Today's perennial producers are faced with stricter crop specifications from their customers, especially if they are suppliers for garden centers or mass merchandisers. Most crop specifications directly apply to the plant's appearance. With increasing competition and an emphasis on plant quality from our customers, we're all expected to step up to the plate and deliver the best products we can.

The height of a plant probably has the most effect on the perceived quality of our products. Plants produced within certain height specifications for their variety will usually be of the highest quality and the most salable. Besides these quality-related attributes, growers 'who grow within the specs,' will often experience other benefits such as less shrinkage, a longer shelf life both in the greenhouse and at the retail site, and the ability to ship more plants per load.

One of the best and most underutilized (perhaps misunderstood) tools to control plant height is the use of chemical plant growth regulators (PGRs). Many have coined the use of growth regulators as both an art and a science. Because of the perceived difficulty of use, many growers aren't comfortable using PGRs. Many growers have either had bad

Leucanthemum 'Marconi' displays a classic Cycocel injury. Many growers tank mix Cycocel and B-Nine using a lower rate of Cycocel and eliminate the phytotoxicity that high rates of Cycocel can cause.
Photos by Paul Pilon.

experiences with these chemicals (overcontrol) or haven't achieved the results they were looking for (undercontrol).

Rest assured that we all have something to learn when implementing these tools into our production programs. We all can be artists if we understand what it is we're trying to create and what we're using to create it. Follow the ground rules and adjust them to fit your crops and growing conditions. When all the factors are taken into consideration, as in science, the results can be duplicated again and again.

Plant growth regulators help growers to produce high quality plants of a desired shape and size. They should be used to regulate the plant's growth, or internode elongation, throughout the growing cycle and not as an effort to stop plant growth when the plants reach a salable size. They are primarily utilized as foliar applications. Regardless of the PGR used, the chemical rates and their results will vary with climate, season, genetics, stage of development, application method, application volume, and the applicator.

Keys to Successful PGR Application

Choose a PGR

Once you decide you need to apply a growth regulator to control plant height of a particular plant species, determine which chemicals the species is responsive to. If there are multiple choices, use the chemical with which you have the most experience and are most comfortable using.

Determine a rate

It's important to determine the rate of the chemical to apply. If you get outside information, you must consider the source. For example, the rates applied in Florida are usually at least twice the concentration of the rates commonly applied in Michigan. If growers in Michigan applied the Florida-based rates, they'd almost certainly obtain too much height control, which could result in unsalable plants. Always remember to translate rates obtained from outside sources to rates that are more relevant to your production site.

When determining the rate, always start at a low concentration and increase it if the level of control is insufficient. It's easier to reapply at the same or a slightly higher concentration than it is to reverse the effects of a chemical overdose. Usually the applications should be seven to ten days apart and consist of the same rate as the first application. It may take ten to twenty days to see the full effect of the PGR applications; therefore, be careful to not judge the effectiveness too early. If the rate needs to be adjusted for a crop, make those changes on the next crop cycle after you're sure there haven't been satisfactory results from the additional applications. Usually raise the rate by no more than 25% at any time. For example, if unsatisfactory results were achieved using a 100-ppm solution, consider increasing the rate for the next crop cycle to 125 ppm.

From my experience, regardless of the crop, it's usually better to apply PGRs at a lower concentration more frequently than it is to apply one higher-rate application. Building PGRs into the development of the plant will provide a cumulative effect within the plant and provide for uniform control of growth, leading to a balanced and aesthetically pleasing plant appearance.

Know your volume

This is probably the most important aspect of applying growth regulators. The volume of spray solution applied over an area has a greater affect on the results than does the concentration of the solution. For

On the left, *Hemerocallis* 'Stella d'Oro' with no PGR applications. The middle plant is shown after three applications of A-Rest at 25 ppm each. The plant on the far right had one drench of A-Rest at 4 ppm.

example, a grower who applies a 5-ppm solution at a volume of 2 qt. per 100 sq. ft. would achieve nearly the same results from applying a 10-ppm solution at a volume of 1 qt. per 100 sq. ft.

For foliar applications, the usual recommendation is to apply 2 qt. of spray solution over 100 sq. ft. of production space. Applying less spray solution usually leads to inadequate coverage and results. Conversely, applying more than 2 qt. per 100 sq. ft. could provide too much control, possibly stunting plant growth.

Another example of the effect of spray volume: A grower intended to apply a 5 ppm solution at the recommended volume of 2 qt. per 100 sq. ft., but due to applicator error and the calibration of the equipment, applied 4 qt. per 100 sq. ft. This over-application resulted in the equivalent of a single 10-ppm application. When the volume is doubled, the intended concentration is also doubled.

Ensure proper coverage

The right volume may be used, but it may not be very effective unless the proper coverage is achieved. By uniform coverage, it's implied that the appropriate volume must thoroughly cover the leaves of the crop. In most cases, smaller droplet sizes should be applied. Always apply PGRs to crops by applying them from two different directions to insure optimal coverage of the leaves and stems. Make a first pass over the crop from one side of the bench, and a second pass from the other side. If this isn't possible, spray on your way down the aisle and again on your way back. This will increase the surface area being treated and increase the activity of the application.

Practice for success

To achieve uniform, consistent, and predictable spray volumes, have the applicator practice using clear water. Choose a known area such as a 1,000-sq. ft. bench. Determine the amount of solution to be applied to this area to satisfy the recommendation of 2 qt. per 100 sq. ft. Apply at the same pressure as the actual application will be, usually between 50 to 250 psi. If not enough solution is distributed over this area, have the applicator slow down his or her walking speed or slightly increase the pressure. If too much is applied, have them increase walking pace or slightly decrease the pressure. The applicator needs to pay attention to how fast he or she is walking, the appearance of the solution leaving the

On the right, *Hosta* 'Royal Standard' after a 4-ppm drench of A-Rest. The plant on the left had no PGR applications.

spray gun, and the amount and size of droplets on the plants. It's also important to learn to make any necessary adjustments during the application and to practice several times they're confident the application of growth regulators will be consistent every time.

Time applications properly

PGRs have the greatest affect on young, actively growing plant tissue. When plants are maturing or becoming reproductive, the application of PGRs seems to have less of an effect on controlling plant height. Many operations decide to use PGRs at the end of a crop cycle just prior to shipping. It's often an application out of panic, thinking their plants will soon be unshippable. The rates and volumes necessary to stop plant growth at this stage are much higher, and the results are often disappointing as compared to the rates required to "regulate" the growth during the production cycle.

Repeat applications as necessary. In most cases, I apply two applications of a PGR to any given crop that requires them. Evaluate the need for a PGR application on a weekly basis, from the beginning of the crop until it's sold. Determine the level of control achieved from previous applications and the need for additional applications. This takes some time and experience. Indicators that some control has been achieved include darker green leaves, a more horizontal or flatter leaf orientation, and shorter internodes.

For the best control, apply the applications seven to ten days apart. Most perennials require two to three applications of PGRs. If you find you're applying four or more times to any particular crop, consider increasing the concentration, increasing the volume, changing chemicals, or adjusting the crop's scheduling.

Evaluate your results

Take good notes as to what worked well and what did not. Don't rely on your memory: Most of us can't remember things we did yesterday, let alone a year ago. Begin PGR use on new varieties on a small scale and don't start on a large scale until you're familiar with the potential outcome. Always set aside some plants that don't get treated to provide an indicator as to the effectiveness of the applications being made. This is very important, especially when first learning how to use PGRs.

Narrow your choices

To make life simpler, limit your PGR use to two or three chemicals at any given time. When using only a couple PGRs at a time, you can gain experience and get comfortable using them in a shorter period of time as compared to using many of these height-control tools simultaneously. Realistically, a majority of your needs can be met by using only three PGRs. Pick the ones you are most comfortable with and that give you the best results under your growing conditions.

Putting It Together

Using these steps will help reduce application error and increase the consistency of your results and your satisfaction. It's very important to have realistic expectations as to what using PGRs will provide. Typically, a height reduction of 10 to 30% can be achieved when using growth regulators throughout the growing cycle. If more height reduction is accomplished, it usually will come with some negative side effects such as stunting, persistence in the landscape, and delayed flowering.

By integrating these guidelines into your production programs, you should, with each application, feel more comfortable and confident using plant growth regulators.

Perennial Plant Growth Regulator Chart

The following chart lists over 150 perennial plant species and the chemical plant growth regulators (PGRs) they are responsive to. Within each plant species, there may be several cultivars that are responsive to the PGRs listed. For example, under the perennial species *Alcea rosea,* there are several cultivars such as 'Chater's Double Hybrids', 'Nigra', and 'Powderpuffs Mixture' (to name a few), which are all responsive to the listed PGRs. For the sake of space, it wasn't possible to list each cultivar for every plant species.

Generally it's safe to assume that all cultivars within a species will respond to the PGRs listed. *Alcea pallida* is altogether a different species than and may or may not be responsive to the same chemicals as *Alcea rosea.* Do not assume what provides height control for one species will also provide height control for another species.

The rates listed are rates commonly applied to perennials in Michigan. These are northern rates; they will need to be adjusted to fit your growing conditions. Typically, southern rates are double the northern application rates. Crop stage of development, spray volume applied, and other factors will influence the results of any PGR application. Use the rates listed as a starting point or as an indication that a particular PGR is effective at controlling height of that plant species, not necessarily the rates you need to apply to achieve adequate height control under your growing conditions.

Quite often there are several PGRs listed for a plant species. When deciding which one to use in your operation, pick the one you are the most comfortable using. Then determine what rate to use in your region of the country. To optimize height control, generally it requires two to three applications using the appropriate rate at seven- to ten-day intervals. The most benefit is achieved by applying PGRs during active growth and not after the crop is nearly overgrown. Monitor your crop's height control needs on a weekly basis.

Set realistic expectations as to the results you are looking for. Under normal circumstances two or three applications will reduce plant height by 15 to 30%. This level of control will typically last two to four weeks before the plant will resume to more normal elongation (growth) rates. Care must be taken and these chemicals must be used in a responsible manner. Growers who overapply these products will most likely decrease plant quality and distribute plants to the consumer that will be slow to resume normal growth in the landscape.

This is probably the largest single source of PGR information for perennials available today. As complete as I have tried to be, I'm sure that other PGR options may exist for each species listed and for several species not listed. If you have information you are willing to share, please contact me so that this list can be updated and redistributed to growers in the future. It is not my intention to endorse any single product, but to provide accurate information growers can implement into production at their discretion. Please send any comments or information to pjpexpress@juno.com.

Advanced Height Control: Tank Mixes

Chemical companies, universities, and growers have recently begun to investigate combining PGRs to enhance the effectiveness of these chemicals on certain perennial varieties. While growers generally apply a single PGR to a crop, there are several species that respond better to tank mixes of two or more PGRs.

If you're new to perennials or PGRs, I'd recommend using the traditional, single-product applications first. For those varieties that don't respond to these controls, consider looking at tank mixes to get a better height reduction. (See p. 56 of this book for a complete article on tank mixes and perennials.)

Test tank mixes on a small scale before you make any major applications. *Remember: There isn't a single growth regulator or a magical combination tank mix that will control plant height on all varieties.*

Perennial Plant Growth Regulators Exposed: Options for This Millennium (All rates shown are for foliar applications)											
Variety	A-Rest (ppm)	B-Nine (ppm)	Bonzi (ppm)	Cycocel (ppm)	Florel (ppm)	Sumagic (ppm)	B-Nine + Sumagic (ppm)	B-Nine + Cycocel (ppm)	A-Rest + B-Nine (ppm)	B-Nine + Bonzi (ppm)	A-Rest + Sumagic (ppm)
Achillea 'Coronation Gold'		2,500	30		500	5					
Achillea filipendulina		2,500	30		500	5					
Achillea millefolium		2,500	30			5	1,875/3	2,500/ 1,000			

(continued)

Perennial Plant Growth Regulators *(continued)*

Variety	A-Rest (ppm)	B-Nine (ppm)	Bonzi (ppm)	Cycocel (ppm)	Florel (ppm)	Sumagic (ppm)	B-Nine + Sumagic (ppm)	B-Nine + Cycocel (ppm)	A-Rest + B-Nine (ppm)	B-Nine + Bonzi (ppm)	A-Rest + Sumagic (ppm)
Achillea 'Moonshine'		2,500	30								
Aconitum napellus							1,875/3				
Aegopodium podagraria		2,500									
Agastache 'Blue Fortune'		2,500				5	1,875/3	2,500/ 1,000			
Ajuga reptans						5					
Alcea rosea	10	2,500	15	1,250	500	<2.5					
Anthemis hybrida tinctoria		2,500				5	1,875/3	2,500/ 1,000			
Aquilegia alpina, A. caerulea, A. chrysantha, A. vulgaris		2,500	30	1,250			1,875/3	2,500/ 1,000	10/ 1,875	1,875/ 15	15/3
Arabis blepharophylla		2,500									
Arabis caucasica		2,500									
Artemesia arborescens		2,500					1,875/3				
Artemesia ludoviciana		2,500					1,875/3				
Artemesia schmidtiana		2,500	30				1,875/3	2,500/ 1,000			
Aruncus aethusifolius							1,875/3				
Asclepias tuberosa	25	2,500	30			5					
Aster frikartii		2,500	30								
Aster tongolensis		2,500					1,875/3				
Astilbe arendsii		2,500	30			5					
Astilbe chinensis, A. japonica						5					
Aubrieta deltoidea		2,500									
Aurinia saxatilis		2,500									
Bellis perennis		2,500				5	1,875/3				
Boltonia asteroides		2,500				5	1,875/3		10/ 1,875		
Buddleia davidii	25		30			5					
Campanula carpatica	25	2,500	10	750		2.5					

(continued)

Perennial Plant Growth Regulators (continued)

Variety	A-Rest (ppm)	B-Nine (ppm)	Bonzi (ppm)	Cycocel (ppm)	Florel (ppm)	Sumagic (ppm)	B-Nine + Sumagic (ppm)	B-Nine + Cycocel (ppm)	A-Rest + B-Nine (ppm)	B-Nine + Bonzi (ppm)	A-Rest + Sumagic (ppm)
Campanula glomerata		2,500	30	500		5					
Campanula medium		2,500					2,000/5		10/ 1,875		
Campanula persicifolia	25	2,500	30			5	1,875/3				
Centaurea dealbata						5					
Centaurea macrocephala						5					
Centaurea montana	25	2,500	30			5	1,875/3				
Centranthus ruber						5					
Cerastium tomentosum						5					
Ceratostigma plumbaginoides		2,500	30	1,250		5					
Chelone glabra			30			5					
Cimicifuga ramosa						5					
Coreopsis grandiflora	25	2,500	30	1,250		5	1,875/3	2,500/ 1,000	10/ 1,875	1,875/ 15	
Coreopsis rosea		2,500				5					
Coreopsis 'Tequila Sunrise'						5					
Coreopsis verticillata		2,500				5	1,875/3	2,500/ 1,000			
Delphinium— Belladonna group						5	2,000/5				
Delphinium elatum	25–50		30			5	2,000/5				
Delphinium grandiflorum			30			5	2,000/5	2,500/ 1,000		2,000/ 30	
Delphinium— Pacific Giant group			30			5	2,000/5			2,000/ 30	
Dendranthema zawadskii		2,500	30			5		2,500/ 1,000			
Dianthus barbatus		3,750	45			10	2,000/5				
Dianthus caryophyllus		2,500	30				2,000/5		10/ 1,875		

(continued)

Perennial Plant Growth Regulators (continued)

Variety	A-Rest (ppm)	B-Nine (ppm)	Bonzi (ppm)	Cycocel (ppm)	Florel (ppm)	Sumagic (ppm)	B-Nine + Sumagic (ppm)	B-Nine + Cycocel (ppm)	A-Rest + B-Nine (ppm)	B-Nine + Bonzi (ppm)	A-Rest + Sumagic (ppm)
Dianthus deltoides				1,250		5	2,000/5				
Dicentra eximia		2,500									
Dicentra formosa		2,500									
Dicentra spectabilis	25	2,500	30			5	1,875/3				
Dicentra 'Zestful'							1,875/3				
Digitalis ambigua						5	1,875/3				
Digitalis x mertonensis						5					
Digitalis purpurea			30			5					
Doronicum orientale	25	2,500	30			5	1,875/3	2,500/ 1,000	10/ 1,875	1,875/ 15	
Echinacea purpurea	25	2,500	30	1,250	500	5	2,000/5	2,000/ 1,000			
Echinops ritro						5	1,875/3				
Erigeron speciosus							1,875/3				
Erysimum cheiri						5					
Eupatorium rugosum						10	2,000/5				
Euphorbia polychroma		2,500									
Fallopia japonica						5					
Gaillardia aristata		2,500	45		500	10	2,000/5	2,500/ 1,000	10/ 1,875	2,000/ 30	15/3
Gaillardia grandiflora								2,500/ 1,000	10/ 1,875		
Galium odoratum				1,250							
Gaura lindheimeri		2,500	30		500	5	1,875/3	2,500/ 1,000		1,875/ 15	
Geranium endressii						5	1,875/3				
Geranium himalayense		2,500	30	1,250	500	5					
Geranium macrorrhizum						5	1,875/3				
Geranium magnificum						5	1,875/3				
Geum chiloense			30				1,875/3			1,875/ 15	
Geum coccineum	25		30	1,250		5					

(continued)

Perennial Plant Growth Regulators *(continued)*

Variety	A-Rest (ppm)	B-Nine (ppm)	Bonzi (ppm)	Cycocel (ppm)	Florel (ppm)	Sumagic (ppm)	B-Nine + Sumagic (ppm)	B-Nine + Cycocel (ppm)	A-Rest + B-Nine (ppm)	B-Nine + Bonzi (ppm)	A-Rest + Sumagic (ppm)
Goniolimon tataricum		2,500									
Helenium autumnale		2,500	30								
Heliopsis helianthoides		2,500			500	5		2,500/1,000			
Hemerocallis (most varieties)	50		60			10	2,000/5	2,500/1,000			
Heuchera micrantha						5					
Heuchera sanguinea		30				5					
Hibiscus moscheutos				1,250		5		2,500/1,000			
Hosta fortunei						10	2,000/5				
Hosta nigrescens						10	2,000/5				
Hosta plantaginea	25	2,500				10	2,000/5	2,500/1,000	10/1,875	2,000/30	
Hosta sieboldiana						10	2,000/5				
Hosta undulata						5	1,875/3				
Iberis sempervirens	25		30			5	1,875/3				
Kniphofia uvaria						5					
Lamiastrum galeobdolon						5					
Lamium maculatum				30	1,250	5					
Lavandula angustifolia, L. officinalis	25	2,500	30			5					
Lavandula intermedia		2,500	30			5		2,500/1,000			
Leucanthemum—Superbum group	25		30			5	1,875/3		10/1,875	1,875/15	
Liatris spicata	25	2,500			750		2,000/5				
Ligularia dentata						5					
Lilium (Asiatic lily)			10			2.5–5					
Lilium 'Star Gazer'						5					
Linum perenne	25	2,500	30			5					
Lobelia cardinalis	25	2,500	30	1,250		5					

(continued)

Perennial Plant Growth Regulators *(continued)*

Variety	A-Rest (ppm)	B-Nine (ppm)	Bonzi (ppm)	Cycocel (ppm)	Florel (ppm)	Sumagic (ppm)	B-Nine + Sumagic (ppm)	B-Nine + Cycocel (ppm)	A-Rest + B-Nine (ppm)	B-Nine + Bonzi (ppm)	A-Rest + Sumagic (ppm)
Lobelia fulgens			30			5					
Lunaria annua						2.5					
Lupinus polyphyllus	25	2,500				5					
Lychnis chalcedonica						5					
Lychnis coronaria		2,500	30		500	5					
Lysimachia clethroides						5					
Lythrum salicaria		2,500				5					
Monarda didyma	25	2,500	30		500	5	1,875/3	2,500/1,000			
Myosotis sylvatica						5					
Nepeta faassenii		2,500	30		500	5	1,875/3	2,500/1,000	10/1,875		
Nepeta subsessilis							2,000/5				
Pachysandra terminalis							1,875/3				
Papaver orientale		2,500									
Paeonia lactiflora						2.5					
Penstemon digitalis 'Husker Red'						5	1,875/3				
Penstemon 'Garnet'	25	2,500		1,250		5					
Perovskia atriplicifolia	25	2,500	30	1,250	500	5	1,875/3	2,500/1,000			
Phlox carolina							2,000/5				
Phlox paniculata		2,500	30			5	1,875/3				
Physalis franchetii						2.5					
Physostegia virginiana					500		1,875/3				
Platycodon grandiflorus			30			5	1,875/3				
Polemonium caeruleum		2,500	30			5	1,875/3	2,500/1,000		1,875/15	15/3
Primula polyantha						5					
Ranunculus repens		2,500					1,875/3				
Rudbeckia fulgida	3,750		60			10	2,000/5	2,500/1,000			

(continued)

Perennial Plant Growth Regulators (continued)

Variety	A-Rest (ppm)	B-Nine (ppm)	Bonzi (ppm)	Cycocel (ppm)	Florel (ppm)	Sumagic (ppm)	B-Nine + Sumagic (ppm)	B-Nine + Cycocel (ppm)	A-Rest + B-Nine (ppm)	B-Nine + Bonzi (ppm)	A-Rest + Sumagic (ppm)
Rudbeckia hirta		3,750					2,000/5				
Rumex sanguineus						5					
Salvia nemorosa		2,500			500		1,875/3				
Salvia officinalis		2,500									
Salvia superba		2,500	30			5	1,875/3				
Salvia verticillata						5					
Scabiosa caucasica		2,500					1,875/3	2,500/1,000			
Scabiosa columbaria		2,500	30		500	5					
Sedum 'Matrona', 'Frosty Morn'						5					
Sedum spectabile		2,500	30		500	5		2,500/1,000		1,875/15	
Sedum spurium			30			5					
Solidago sphacelata		2,500	30			5					
Stachys byzantina						5					
Stokesia laevis	25	2,500	30	1,250	500	5	1,875/3	2,500/1,000			
Tanacetum—Coccineum group		2,500	30			5					
Veronica longifolia	25	2,500	30	1,250		5		2,500/1,000			
Veronica spicata	25	2,500	30			5		2,500/1,000			
Viola cornuta, V. tricolor						2.5					
Viola obliqua						5					

May 2002

Chapter 4
Forcing and Timing

Manipulating Day Length to Flower Perennials

Erik S. Runkle, Royal D. Heins, Arthur C. Cameron, and William H. Carlson

Perennials in flower sell. The challenge, of course, is to make them flower. Some herbaceous perennials present no problem—just turn up the temperature in the greenhouse in the winter or early spring. However, many species remain vegetative until April or May, even if heated. We're finding that most of these slow starters are actually long-day plants, which are signaled to flower when day lengths reach or exceed a certain point known as their critical photoperiod. These plants flower in response to changes in natural day lengths. By understanding the critical photoperiod for lower induction, growers can manipulate photoperiods to make plants either vegetative or reproductive.

Photoperiods
Natural photoperiods vary during the year and by latitude. Day length is the shortest on December 21 and increases until June 21; thereafter, it decreases. The transition from spring to summer—from short days to long days—initiates flowering in some plants.

The seasonal fluctuation of natural photoperiods becomes more dramatic traveling farther north. For New Orleans (30°N latitude), perceived day length ranges from slightly fewer than 11 hours to slightly more than 14½ hours. In East Lansing, Michigan (43°N latitude), day lengths range from fewer than 10 hours to longer than 16 hours. These day lengths are approximately thirty-five to forty minutes longer than the time from sunrise to sundown because plants perceive light before sunrise and after sunset.

Photoperiods can be created in the greenhouse, an already common practice with poinsettias and chrysanthemums. Short days are created by pulling black cloth or plastic over plants to limit the day length. For poinsettias, which are short-day plants, black cloth is used in northern areas to induce flowering. Long days can be created by lighting (greater than 10 f.c.) either at the end of the day (known as day-extension lighting) or for several hours during the middle of the night (known as night-interruption lighting). Night-interruption lighting commonly is used to keep mums vegetative.

These same techniques can be applied to herbaceous perennials. A long-day plant will remain vegetative under short days. The same plant will be induced to flower when given photoperiods equal to or longer than its critical photoperiod. Within a given species, like mums, for example, there may be different critical photoperiods. Be careful not to assume that cultivars of the same species will respond identically to the same photoperiod.

Photoperiod Experiments

At Michigan State University, we are studying photoperiod and how it influences flowering of many herbaceous perennials. Plants were grown in a greenhouse at a constant 68°F from either uncooled plugs or plugs that received fifteen weeks of 41°F. The photoperiods were ten, twelve, fourteen, sixteen, or twenty-four hours or a nine-hour day with a four-hour night interruption. Plants were discarded if there was no visible bud after one hundred days in the greenhouse.

A summary of some of the results of this experiment is given in the table. The recommendations are based on the percentage of plants that flowered and the time it took them to flower. A "Yes" in the cold treatment column indicates plants either benefit from or require a period of cold before forcing. An "N/Y" means plants responded to photoperiod the same way with or without a cold treatment.

Based on the experiment, herbaceous perennials that grow in most northern climates can be grouped into three categories based on photoperiodic effects on flowering: obligate long-day, facultative long-day, and day-neutral plants. An obligate long-day plant will not flower without long days and then only when the day length exceeds its critical photoperiod. For example, *Coreopsis verticillata* 'Moonbeam' did not flower under twelve-hour or shorter photoperiods. All 'Moonbeam' plants grown under photoperiods of at least fourteen hours or night interruption flowered uniformly.

Facultative long-day plants flower under short days but more rapidly under long days. Long days thus are beneficial, but not required, for

The Effect of Photoperiod on Flowering of Selected Perennials

Species	Recommendation		Flowering Percentage					
	Night interruption*	Cold treatment**	Photoperiod					
			10	12	14	16	24	NI
Long days required								
Asclepias tuberosa	Yes	Yes						
Campanula carpatica 'Blue Clips'	Yes	N/Y						
Gaillardia x *grandiflora* 'Goblin'	Yes	Yes						
Coreopsis verticillata 'Moonbeam'	Yes	N/Y						
Hibiscus x *hybrida* 'Disco Belle Mixed'	Yes	No						
Gypsophila paniculata 'Double Snowflake'	Yes	Yes						
Oenothera missouriensis	Yes	Yes						
Echinacea purpurea 'Bravado'	Yes	Yes						
Long days beneficial								
Physostegia virginiana 'Alba'	Yes	Yes						
Lobelia x *speciosa* 'Compliment Scarlet'	Yes	Yes						
Salvia x *superba* 'Blue Queen'	Yes	Yes						
No response to long days								
Armeria x *hybrida* 'Dwarf Ornament Mix'	No	No						
Armeria latifolia	No	Yes						
Lavendula angustifolia 'Munstead Dwarf'	No	Yes						
Scabiosa columbaria 'Butterfly Blue'	No	N/Y						
Veronica longifolia 'Sunny Border Blue'	No	Yes						
Veronica spicata 'Blue'	No	Yes						

*Yes = four-hour night interruption is recommended,
 No = no benefit from night interruption.
**Yes = ten to fifteen weeks of cold treatment is recommended,
 N/Y = plants respond the same way to photoperiod
    with or without cold,
 No = cold treatment not recommended.

Legend:
- 0% flowered
- 1 to 33% flowered
- 35 to 66% flowered
- 67 to 99% flowered
- 100% flowered

flowering. An example of a facultative long-day plant is *Salvia* x *superba* 'Blue Queen'. After a period of cold treatment, plants flower upon exposure to warm temperatures. However, plants flower faster as the duration of the photoperiod increases. Plants averaged fifty-eight days to flower

Coreopsis verticillata 'Moonbeam' did not flower under twelve-hour or shorter photoperiods.

under ten-hour photoperiods but only thirty days under photoperiods of at least sixteen hours or night interruption.

Day-neutral plants flower regardless of photoperiod at the same time; long days are not beneficial. An example of a day-neutral plant is *Veronica longifolia* 'Sunny Border Blue'. *Veronica longifolia* relies on other environmental signals to initiate flowering, such as warm temperatures following exposure to a period of cold treatment.

Although there is no clear-cut division between short and long days, the long-day plants in this study normally remained vegetative when there were fewer than twelve hours of light per day. They all flowered quickly when there were more than fourteen or fifteen hours of light per day. Few long-day plants flowered with twelve hours of light per day, and those that did took longer.

A long-day plant actually perceives the duration of darkness, not

Salvia x superba 'Blue Queen' is a facultative long-day plant: After cold treatment, plants flower under all photoperiods but long days accelerate flowering.

light, in each twenty-four-hour cycle. An obligate long-day plant flowers only when the uninterrupted duration of darkness is *less* than a critical value. Short day with night-interruption lighting is equally effective as a long-day extension because the critical night length is not reached. To keep an obligate long-day plant vegetative, the uninterrupted duration of *darkness* must exceed some value, usually twelve to fourteen hours for many perennials.

Photoperiod is just one environmental signal that initiates flowers of herbaceous perennials. Some perennials require only inductive photoperiods and warm temperatures to flower. Others have one or more requirements that must be met. For example, some species have a juvenile stage during which plants will not respond to flower-inductive conditions until they grow a certain number of leaves (or nodes). Furthermore, many plants require or benefit from a period of cold before forcing under warm temperatures.

As these flowering components are discovered, they can be integrated to form a schedule for bringing a given species into flower. As schedules are developed, perennial growers will be able to bring a wide range of perennials to flower on any desired date. In the meantime, the table provides pertinent photoperiod information for bringing selected herbaceous perennials into flower.

June 1996

Perennials: Best Long-Day Treatments for Your Varieties

Cheryl K. Hamaker, Royal Heins, Art Cameron, and Will Carlson

In the greenhouse industry, growers often use photoperiod manipulation to shorten or lengthen natural day lengths to obtain vegetative or reproductive growth. When days are naturally short, you can provide long-days by lighting in the middle of the night (night interruption lighting) or by lighting before or after the natural day (predawn or day-extension lighting). Like in poinsettia and chrysanthemum production, you can use lighting to create long days to induce flowering in long-day herbaceous perennials. In our experiment at Michigan State University, we wanted to determine how different lighting strategies compared for inducing consistent flowering in several herbaceous perennials. Keep in mind that short-day and long-day plants respond differently to photoperiodic lighting. Most short-day plants remain vegetative in response to relatively short periods of night interruption lighting. However, most long-day plants require night breaks of at least several hours for uniform and consistent flowering.

Traditionally, long days used to prevent flowering in poinsettias and mums have been delivered as a four-hour night interruption with incandescent lamps. We've generally found that a four-hour night interruption also induces flowering in long-day herbaceous perennials. Alternatively, fourteen- to sixteen-hour day lengths provided by day extension also induce rapid uniform flowering (see the article "Manipulating Day Length to Flower Perennials" on p. 79).

We grew plants in the greenhouse at a constant 68°F after receiving either zero or twelve weeks of 41°F. Plants were forced under a nine-hour short-day or one of five long-day lighting strategies for twelve weeks. The five long-day lighting methods include a seven-hour day extension, a four-hour night interruption, a seven-hour predawn extension and twenty-four-hour continuous light. All treatments received nine-hour natural day length before black cloth was pulled. All long-day treatments were delivered by incandescent lamps that provided a minimum of 10 f.c.

In this experiment, each long-day lighting strategy induced flowering, but some lighting treatments were more effective than others for some species (see table). Factors such as flowering percentage, time to flower, and bud number at first flower were influenced by the long-day delivery strategy. In general, a seven-hour predawn treatment was less effective than other long-day treatments for inducing flowering. For example, flowering percentage for *Asclepias tuberosa* grown under the seven-hour predawn treatment was low compared to plants grown under the other long-day treatments (figure 1).

Long-day delivery method affected time to flower in both *Coreopsis grandiflora* 'Early Sunrise' and *Leucanthemum* x *superbum* 'Snow Lady'. Flowering was delayed approximately fourteen days in *Coreopsis* grown under seven-hour predawn treatments compared to plants grown under other long-day treatments either with or without a cold treatment (figure 2). Time to flower for *Leucanthemum* was also delayed

A plus sign (+) indicates faster or grater flowering percentage, while a minus sign (-) indicates delay or smaller flowering percentage compared to that of plants in other treatments (blank cells).

Species	Flowering	Four-hour night interruption	Seven-hour night interruption	Seven-hour day extension	Seven-hour predawn treatments	24-hour
Achillea filipendulina		**No cold**				
	Days to first flower					
	Flowering percentage	No flowering without cold				
		12 weeks at 41°F				
	Days to first flower		+		−	+
	Flowering percentage				−	+
Asclepias tuberosa		**No cold**				
	Days to first flower	No significant difference				
	Flowering percentage		+		−	+
		12 weeks at 41°F				
	Days to first flower	Not tested				
	Flowering percentage					
Campanula carpatica		**No cold**				
	Days to first flower					−
	Flowering percentage	No significant difference				
		12 weeks at 41°F				
	Days to first flower			−		
	Flowering percentage	No significant difference				
Coreopsis grandiflora		**No cold**				
	Days to first flower				+	−
	Flowering percentage	No significant difference				
		12 weeks at 41°F				
	Days to first flower				−	+
	Flowering percentage	No significant difference				
Leucanthemum x superbum		**No cold**				
	Days to first flower	No significant difference				
	Flowering percentage	No significant difference				
		12 weeks at 41°F				
	Days to first flower	Not tested				
	Flowering percentage					
Salvia superba		**No cold**				
	Days to first flower	No significant difference				
	Flowering percentage	No significant difference				
		12 weeks at 41°F				
	Days to first flower	No significant difference				
	Flowering percentage	No significant difference				

approximately ten days when plants were grown under seven-hour predawn treatments. Finally, final inflorescence number was reduced in both *Campanula carpatica* 'Blue Clips' and 'Early Sunrise' when grown under the seven-hour predawn treatment compared to other long-day delivery methods.

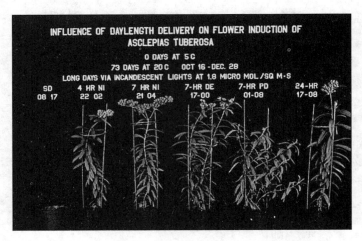

Figure 1. Flowering percentage of *Asclepias tuberosa* was affected by long-day lighting strategies. Only 40% flowering occurred for plants grown under a seven-hour predawn extension. Plants initiated buds under this treatment; however, buds were aborted before first flower.

Figure 2. *Coreopsis grandiflora* 'Early Sunrise' doesn't require cold in order to flower. However, time to flower for *Coreopsis* was delayed ten days in plants grown under a seven-hour predawn extension compared to other long-day treatments.

Plant response to long-day treatments was also affected by cold treatment. Cooling often decreases the minimum photoperiod required for flowering of many long-day plants. We found that flowering was significantly delayed in uncooled 'Blue Clips' grown under twenty-four-hour continuous lighting: following a cold treatment, flowering was no longer delayed (figures 3 and 4). As mentioned previously, flowering of coreopsis grown under seven-hour predawn treatment was delayed on cooled and uncooled plants. However, the delay in time to flower was reduced approximately seven days on cooled plants.

Figure 3. A cold treatment isn't necessary for flowering of *Campanula carpatica* 'Blue Clips'. However, without a cold treatment, flowering is delayed significantly (approximately thirty days) when plants are grown under twenty-four-hour continuous lighting.

This experiment shows the variation in response of herbaceous perennials to different long-day delivery techniques. Overall, both night-interruption and day-extension treatments were superior to predawn treatments for most species tested. In addition, a four-hour night interruption was horticulturally similar to both a seven-hour day extension and a seven-hour night interruption for supplying long days to induce flowering because plants actually perceive the duration of darkness, rather than light, in each daily cycle.

For flowering to be induced in a long-day plant, the length of the dark period must be less than a critical value. For example, if a plant has a critical photoperiod of sixteen hours, it actually requires a period of darkness equal to or less than eight hours. So, even though plants grown

Figure 4. After a cold treatment, flowering of *Campanula carpatica* 'Blue Clips' was no longer delayed when grown under twenty-four-hour continuous lighting. All plants flowered quickly and uniformly, regardless of long-day lighting strategy.

under a seven-hour day extension receive three hours more light than those grown under a four-hour night interruption, the uninterrupted period of darkness for both long-day treatments is less than the critical value required for flowering.

You can use a variety of methods to provide long days in the greenhouse to force herbaceous perennials effectively. Certainly, plants will flower under the natural long days of the summer; so what's the best way to provide long days under naturally short days? The results of this experiment show that both seven-hour day extensions and four-hour night interruptions can be equally effective during the middle of winter when days are shortest. However, the four-hour night interruption requires less electricity because plants are lit for three fewer hours each night. During the longer days of spring, the difference in electrical usage disappears because the duration of a day extension only needs to be long enough to provide a sixteen-hour photoperiod.

We suggest a four-hour night interruption to provide long days to herbaceous perennials. If electric service to your greenhouse is inadequate to light all the plants you want to light simultaneously, we suggest that you light part of the plants as a day extension so the total day length is sixteen hours. Light the remainder of the plants with a night interruption. If electrical services are still inadequate, lighting before sunrise to provide a sixteen-hour day will promote flowering, but plants may not flower as quickly as plants lit with day extension or night interruption.

Editor's Note: The authors would like to thank industry supporters who made the research discussed in this article possible, as well as Erik Runkle, Cara Wallace, and Tom Wallace.

November 1996

Perennial Flower Induction—The Light You Use Can Make a Difference

Catherine Whitman, Royal Heins, Arthur Cameron, and William Carlson

While lighting systems for short-day plants are common, few horticultural crops are long-day plants, and little information exists on effective lighting systems for them. In preliminary experiments at Michigan State University, we've used "mum lighting" successfully to induce flowering in many perennial species. However, the actual required light intensity was unknown. In addition, some reports have said light sources effective for controlling development of short-day plants may not work well for long-day plants.

Several important horticultural crops, including poinsettias and chrysanthemums, are short-day plants. Controlling day length provides a convenient way to influence the development of plants that respond to photoperiod. Growers frequently use lighting to lengthen photoperiod and prevent flowering in short-day plants. Supplemental lights can be turned on in the middle of the night, often from 10 P.M. to 2 A.M., or for several hours after sunset. Light intensities required are much lower than those needed for photosynthesis. This "mum lighting" is usually provided with incandescent lamps at 10 f.c.

Experiments have shown that many perennials are long-day plants. Some species will never flower unless day lengths are longer than the critical photoperiod; others just flower more rapidly when photoperiods are longer.

In select species of perennials, we found that providing a least 10 f.c. will successfully induce flowering. While 5 f.c. is adequate to flower all species, we recommend designing for at least 10 f.c. to compensate for uneven lighting, variability within the crop, and bulb dimming from lamp age. Standard mum lighting is quite adequate for inducing flowering in the perennial species we researched. Cool white fluorescent, high-pressure sodium, or metal halide lamps are also effective and will result in more compact plants for some plant species.

The first objective of this experiment was to determine the light intensity required to induce flowering in several perennial species. We wanted to establish two values: threshold, or lowest intensity that would induce any flowering, and saturation, or minimum intensity needed for uniform flowering. Our second objective was to compare the effectiveness of several different light sources for flower induction. Incandescent lights are inexpensive to purchase and install, but they emit a relatively large amount of far-red light that promotes stem elongation and reduces branching in many plants. They are also less efficient at converting electricity to light than most other light sources. Cool white fluorescent, high-pressure sodium, or metal halide lamps have the potential to limit plant height and provide savings in energy costs, compared to incandescent lamps. Other lamps can also simplify installation, as fewer fixtures may be required.

Finding the Right Light

We chose four species of herbaceous perennials that require long photoperiods for flowering, but have no requirement for cold treatments: *Campanula carpatica* 'Blue Clips', *Coreopsis grandiflora* 'Early Sunrise', *Coreopsis verticillata* 'Moonbeam', and *Rudbeckia fulgida* 'Goldsturm'. To ensure that plants were vegetative before the experiment

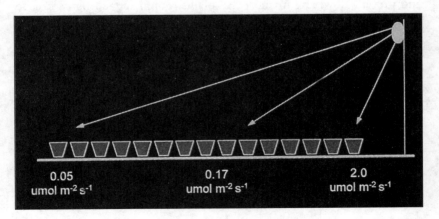

Figure 1. Diagram of light setup on each bench. Plants received 0.25 f.c. (left) to 10 f.c. (right). Lights were on from 5 p.m. until midnight.

began, we received them four weeks after sowing and grew them under a nine-hour photoperiod (short day) for roughly ten weeks before beginning the experiment. We grew all plants at 68°F.

We selected four lamps that are readily available for greenhouse use: cool white fluorescent, high-pressure sodium, incandescent, and metal halide. We installed each light above one end of a bench to create a gradient of light intensity, then lined up fifteen plants of each species along the bench so they received 10 f.c. to 0.25 f.c. of light (figure 1). We pulled blackcloth over the light and benches from 5 P.M. until 8 A.M. to exclude any stray light. Lights were on from 5 P.M. to midnight. We grew a separate group of plants under a nine-hour photoperiod.

None of the plants flowered under a nine-hour photoperiod. We found that *Campanula carpatica, Coreopsis grandiflora,* and *C. verticillata* were very sensitive to low light levels—a few plants of each species treated with light intensities as low as 0.25 f.c. bloomed. Plants treated with higher intensities flowered more quickly. *Campanula carpatica, Coreopsis grandiflora,* and *C. verticillata* plants treated with 5 f.c. flowered at approximately the same time as those treated with 10 f.c. *Rudbeckia fulgida* plants were somewhat less sensitive and didn't flower

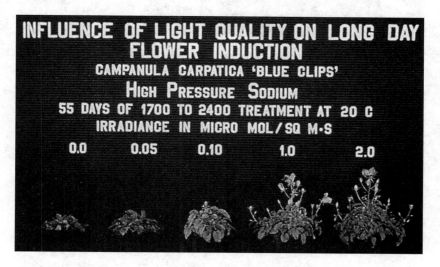

Figure 2. *Campanula carpatica* 'Blue Clips' treated with high-pressure sodium lights. Those treated with 5 f.c. (1.0 micromol/m^2•second) or more flowered at the same time. Flowering was delayed or not induced on plants exposed to lower light intensities-note bud on plant treated with 0.5 f.c. (0.1 micromol/m^2•second).

at light levels below 1 to 2 f.c. *R. fulgida* plants treated with 6 f.c. or more flowered at about the same time.

These response patterns were very similar under all four light sources and for all four species tested. We found no significant differences in time to flower at light intensities above the saturation intensity (figure 3). For *Campanula carpatica* and *Coreopsis grandiflora,* plants treated with incandescent light were significantly taller than those treated with any other lights (figure 4). All *Coreopsis verticillata* and *Rudbeckia fulgida* plants that flowered were essentially the same height.

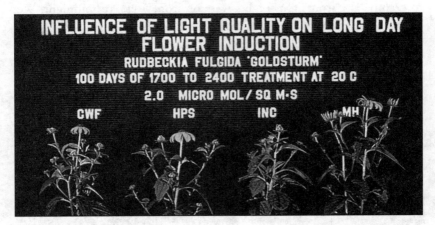

Figure 3. At the 10 f.c. level, time to flower didn't differ significantly among the four light sources we tested.

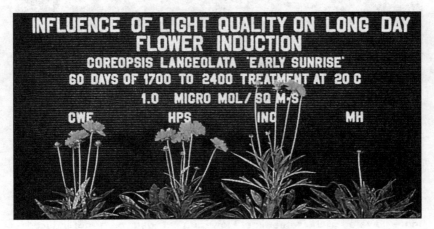

Figure 4. *Coreopsis grandiflora* 'Early Sunrise' plants forced under incandescent lamps were taller than those in other treatments.

The Details

To provide the correct light intensity from incandescent lamps, hang lights 5 ft. above the soil surface. For one 4-ft. bed, hang a single string of 6-watt bulbs spaced 4 ft. apart. For two beds, use a string of 100-watt bulbs 6 ft. apart, for three beds, 150-watt bulbs 6 ft. apart. It's impossible to recommend specific installations of cool white fluorescent, high-pressure sodium, or metal halide lamps due to the variety of fixtures and luminaire (reflector) shapes available. The luminaire shape has a dramatic influence on the spread and intensity of light emitted, so you must design these lighting systems by trial and error. Purchase a light meter and confirm the light intensities provided.

Finished plants are generally more attractive if they're bulked or grown under non-inductive photoperiods for some time before being given long-day treatments. They tend to have more laterals and produce more flowers. Because these species are so sensitive to low levels of light, be careful during the bulking period to avoid exposure to stray light. It will induce premature flowering, particularly if you're using supplemental lighting in an adjacent greenhouse section.

July 1996

Forcing Perennials in the Greenhouse

Allan M. Armitage

The most important aspect for greenhouse production of perennials is the presence of a flower, or at least a flower bud. Unfortunately, North American consumers demand a flower before sales of a species significantly rise. Like it or not, this will not change. While the presence of a flower may not be in the interest of the plant, that's the reality of the marketplace.

Forcing flowers is the single most confusing aspect for people not used to growing perennials. Many (but not all) species require some cold temperatures for best growth and flowering; some (but not all) require photoperiodic treatments; and some (but not all) require growth regulators to maintain a suitable mature height in the container. Proper selection of species and cultivars can help a great deal in simplifying forcing of plants.

Most greenhouse operators are good propagators, but perennial propagation from seed or vegetative tissue is slightly different from germinating impatiens or rooting pot mums. Here are some steps necessary to force selected perennial species in the greenhouse.

Facilities

You'll need propagation facilities for seed and/or cuttings (some light, moisture, and temperature control). This is not as necessary if plugs or rooted cuttings are purchased. A cooler (35 to 40°F) is useful, but not an absolute requirement. Plugs, however, should be either precooled by the plug grower or cooled in a cool greenhouse if a cooler isn't used.

Table 1. Early Spring Forcing

Genus and Species	Common Name	Cultivars
Ajuga reptans	Bugleweed	'Burgundy Glow', 'Bronze Beauty'
Alchemilla mollis	Lady's mantle	
Anchusa sp.	Alkanet	
Aquilegia x *hybrida*	Columbine	'Song Bird' series, 'Musik' series
Arabis albida	Rock cress	'Snow Cap', 'Spring Charm'
Armeria maritima	Sea thrift	'Splendens', 'Vindictive'
Campanula carpatica	Carpathian harebell	'Blue Clips', 'White Clips'
Campanula garganica	Gargano bellflower	
Cerastium tomentosum	Snow in summer	'Silvery Summer'
Dianthus		'Bath's Pink'
Gypsophila repens	Creeping baby's breath	'Rosea, Alba'
Iberis sempervirens	Candytuft	'Snowflake'
Myosotis scorpioides	Forget-me-not	'Indigo Blue', 'Rosea'
Phlox subulata	Creeping phlox	'Emerald Blue', 'Red Delight', etc.
Salvia superba	Perennial sage	'Blue Queen', 'Stradford Blue'
Saxifraga arendsii	Saxifrage	'Purple Robe'
Verbena canadensis	Verbena	'Homestead Purple', 'Silver Anne'

Use a greenhouse or bays with at least two temperature zones, a cold zone at 40 to 50°F (essential if no cooler is available) and a warm zone at 50 to 65°F night temperatures. Supplemental growing lights (such as HID, metal halide) are useful only if they're already in place.

You must have the ability to provide long days during the winter for spring-forced crops. Incandescent lights are sufficient, but metal-halide HID lamps can be used if already in place. Metal-halide lamps are better than sodium lamps for photoperiodic control.

Follow normal fertility and disease/insect prevention techniques.

Species Selection

Early spring forcing

The easiest species to force for early spring are those that normally flower in spring and early summer. In nature their cycle is warm-cold-warm (fall-winter-spring), which is easy to copy in the greenhouse. Table 1 includes a sample of species suitable for early spring forcing. Other species are also very useful for forcing from crowns or for their foliage. Some of these are in table 2.

Table 2. Forcing from Crowns or for Foliage

Genus and Species	Common Name	Cultivars
Astilbe x *arendsii*	Astilbe	'Deutschland', 'Finale', 'Glow', etc.
Hosta sp.	Hosta	Many available
Ajuga reptans	Bugleweed	'Bronze Beauty', 'Burgundy Glow'
Artemisia sp.	Wormword	'Silver Mound', 'Powis Castle'
Sedum spurium	Stonecrop	'Dragon's Blood'
Sempervivum tectorum	Hens and chicks	Mix
Vinca major	Periwinkle	'Variegata'

Other non-perennial but cold-loving species work well in this program and shouldn't be overlooked. They may be sold when weather is still cool but as spring approaches. These species are in table 3.

Table 3. Non-Perennial, Cold-Loving Species

Genus and Species	Common Name	Cultivars
Bellis perennis	English daisy	'Haberna' series
Dianthus (*chinensis* x *barbatus*)	Annual pinks	'Ideal', 'Princess' series
Primula x *polyantha, P. elatior*	Primrose	'Danova', 'Crayon', 'Pageant' series
Viola sp.	Violas	'Princess', 'Jewel', 'Sorbet'

Summer forcing

Many popular perennials such as coreopsis, *Echinacea, Oenothera, Gaillardia, Helianthus, Heliopsis,* etc. are also forcible, but they're best grown in a warm greenhouse (where marigolds and impatiens are grown). Herbs such as lavender can be forced when temperatures are a little warmer. They may be forced for a late spring/early summer program, and while they can be used in an early spring program, they're most useful for a late forcing program. Some of these are in table 4.

Table 4. Summer Forcing

Genus and Species	Common Name	Cultivars
Aster dumosus	Dwarf asters	'Prof Kippenburg', 'Woods' series
Coreopsis grandiflora	Hybrid coreopsis	'Early Sunrise'
Coreopsis auriculata	Mouse-ear coreopsis	'Nana'
Gaillardia aristata	Blanket flower	'Goblin', 'Mandarin'
Oenothera tetragona	Evening primrose	
Platycodon grandiflorum	Balloon flower	'Astra', 'Sentimental Blue'
Heliopsis scabra	Heliopsis	'Summer Sun'
Sedum sp.	Sedum	'Autumn Joy', 'Meteor'

The Need for Cold

Cool temperatures (35 to 40°F) are necessary in some species for seed germination and flower development. Researchers have conducted research in which plugs are cooled in a cooler. At University of Georgia Athens, we found 128 plugs to be a good compromise between sufficient size for responding to cold and dense enough planting for space efficiency. We cooled plugs in a cooler (40°F) for up to twelve weeks, then placed them in the greenhouse for subsequent forcing. Not all plants require cooling for flowering (*Myosotis, Arabis, Aquilegia, Gypsophila*), but *cooling reduced time on the greenhouse bench in every species we tested.*

The amount of time in a cooler should be minimized because of the potential for storage diseases when plants remain too long. In general, we found four to eight weeks' cooling was sufficient, although some plants deteriorated more with eight storage weeks compared to four (*Aquilegia*). We didn't study better cooling techniques to enhance plugs in the cooler at Georgia; therefore, my recommendations are for "standard" coolers.

In the cooler, incandescent lights (about twelve hours) are useful but may not be necessary. The closer to 32°F, the less need for light; the warmer the temperature, the more light required. Lights are simply useful to reduce stress on seedlings so when they're brought out of the cooler they aren't half dead and require two or more weeks on the bench just to recover. Lights are difficult to install in many coolers, so using cooler temperatures is recommended if lights aren't possible. Ten to 15 f.c. appears to be sufficient. Be sure plugs are occasionally watered, as drying out in a well-vented cooler is not uncommon. Some species, such as *Campanula,* and many bulbous crops, such as *Liatris,* may be frozen in the cooler or greenhouse without harm.

Cooling plugs in the greenhouse is also an excellent method. Plugs may be gradually frozen with little loss, and air circulation and light reduce storage diseases to almost none. If plugs are cooled in the greenhouse, they may be cooled for much longer periods of time, particularly if day temperatures rise significantly. This is usually done in northern areas of the country only. In the South, warm day temperatures often negate cool temperatures received during the day.

Growth and Flowering

Many perennial species have evolved to include a period of cold temperatures in their life cycle. This is generally more because of necessity (cold weather) than some preordained genetic sequence. Regardless of magic or science, growers should provide all spring and early summer flowering perennials with a cool greenhouse for growth even if plugs have been precooled.

All crops grown in 4- to 6-in. containers are often better quality when grown cool (35 to 50°F) for a period of time. They're more compact, better branched, and flower more uniformly. The downside is that they're slower to turn over. This is particularly true for many-stemmed plants like *Gypsophila* (baby's breath) and *Cerastium* (Anne-in-summer) and less essential for single-stem plants like *Salvia* and columbine. We've grown many precooled plugs when day temperatures didn't fall below 55°F, night temperatures were 60 to 62°F, and very little stretch occurred.

All biennials (*Dianthus barbatus, Digitalis, Lunaria*) require a cold treatment for flower induction. Gibberellic acid can substitute for the cold, but why mess with it when cold works better anyway?

Warm temperatures are useful near the end of the production cycle, regardless of cooling when flowers must be opened. In general, the longer the period of time below 60°F, the better the quality. However, the colder the temperatures, the longer the time in the greenhouse or the cold frame. *There is no need to freeze crops. In general, foliage is damaged; flowers are delayed, or crops may go into dormancy.* Never reduce temperature below freezing on actively growing crops.

Natural summer- and fall-flowering crops handle warm greenhouse temperatures more easily without loss of quality. Summer species such as *Salvia, Coreopsis, Echinacea,* and all herbs don't require cool greenhouse temperatures for good quality.

Continue cooling finished plants using the cool greenhouse only (no cooling on plugs) for spring-flowering plants for about nine to twelve weeks for best quality growth and flowering. There is no maximum length of time; the time to market dictates the time in the cool greenhouse or cold frame.

The Need for Long Days

Many perennials have evolved to produce flowers as temperatures increase and days get longer. The application of long days is useful to accelerate flowering. This can be done by extending day length, using night break lighting, or cyclic lighting. In general a fourteen- to sixteen-hour day works well for long day perennials, and night break lighting (11 P.M. to 2 A.M.) is also used successfully. The least expensive and the most efficient light source is incandescent lamps because of the red-far-red spectrum they provide. Avoid lights with no red in their spectrum because they aren't as effective. Long days are generally applied after plants have almost filled the container. For a March 15 market date, begin lighting around or slightly after Christmas; for an April 15, around the end of January.

Nearly every plant we've tested flowers faster when subjected to long days. In most cases, flowering is enhanced by long days, but some species such as *Asclepias, Campanula, Catananche,* and *Echinacea must* have long days. One exception to long days usefulness is *Saxifraga,* which appears to be a short day–long day plant, that is, short days are needed to make the plant responsive to long days.

Many of the summer-flowering perennials, particularly daisies, also flower more rapidly with long days, which can be naturally used for a summer and fall forcing program. Although many other perennials also respond to long days, not all are suitable for forcing.

Long Day and Short Day Conditions

Does it make more sense to treat some plants like we do poinsettias and mums, and provide the opposite photoperiod it needs initially, then switch plants to the appropriate photoperiod? In the case of points and mums, we provide long days then switch to short days. In the case of perennials, would there be a benefit to providing short days initially and then long days or even vice versa?

A number of universities (Virginia Tech, Michigan State, Georgia, and others) recently researched long day/short day combinations to see how flowering and plant height would be affected. This is sometimes called limited induction. In general, short days followed by long days help reduce height but cause longer flowering times. Long days followed by short days do much the same thing. Height control can be accomplished with manipulation of photoperiods. If your growing system allows for manipulation of photoperiod, you may see height control with loss of flower quality.

The Need for Heat

As the market date approaches, the greenhouse may have to be heated to 60 to 65°F nights to allow for better nutritional update and more rapid flowering. In general, this occurs two to four weeks prior to market date. You can use warmer temperatures, but plants for the early spring program may stretch, particularly if winter light intensity is low.

Growth Regulators

Most spring-flowering perennials won't require growth regulators, but if day temperatures warm up or light intensities are low, growth regulators are quite useful. The main growth regulator for perennials in the U.S. is B-Nine (85%), which is applied at a rate of 3,000 to 5,000 ppm to columbine, candytuft, forget-me-not, and salvia. Spray when flower stems begin to elongate. Apply Cycocel (750 to 1,500 ppm) to balloon flower, pinks, and English daisy as a drench or a spray. A-Rest, Bonzi, and Sumagic are also used quite effectively. Check labels to be sure chemicals are registered for ornamental flowering crops. Growth regulators are simply tools to help produce a high-quality plant; they need not be used if plant stretch or mature height isn't a problem. Limited induction and DIF have more long-term benefits for height control than chemicals.

Nutritional Needs

When plants are grown cool (less than 40°F), plant growth is slow and nutrient requirements are low. However, cold soils also inhibit nutrient uptake. During cold treatment, apply nitrate type fertilizers (calcium nitrate, potassium nitrate, etc.) rather than fertilizers high in ammonia form of nitrogen (20-20-20, ammonium nitrate, etc.). Approximately 50 to 100 ppm of nitrogen is sufficient when applied at every watering. leach with plain water every fourth to fifth irrigation. Overapplication causes soluble salt buildup, dead roots, and dead plants. At best, over-application can cause stretched plants. Too little fertilizer results in stunted and chlorotic plants. Applications of iron chelate are helpful to many species, particularly *Myosotis*. As temperatures warm up, increase the fertilizer concentration, but stay between 100 to 200 ppm nitrogen. During flowering, reduce the nitrogen application and use potassium nitrate at about 100 ppm nitrogen. Plants will be hardened off before they go to the retail center.

July 1996

Armitage's Perennial Plant Groupings for Flower Forcing

Allan M. Armitage

We classify so many species as perennials that some simplification of their environmental responses is necessary. I have grouped plants we worked with at the University of Georgia into four groups so that production systems can be facilitated. We want to enlarge the list of species under each plant group as we continue our research.

I conducted the vast majority of this work at the University of Georgia and this article only covers those plants we have actually worked with. All of our work was based on 128 or 50-plug tray sizes and grown in southern conditions. If a species or cultivar is not mentioned, it simply means we haven't worked with it, not that it doesn't fit into any of the systems mentioned.

In all groupings, cool temperatures, whether in a cooler or in the greenhouse, are beneficial and recommended. Precooled plugs should be purchased if cooling facilities aren't available.

Group I. Essentially day-neutral, these plants may flower a little faster under long days, but changes in production aren't necessary. *Arabis* 'Spring Charm', 'Snow Cap', 'Compinkie'; *Arabis sturii* (cold necessary); *Armeria maritima, Aubrieta* 'Royal Red', 'Whitewall Gem'; *Erodium reichardii* 'Roseum'; *Platycodon* 'Astra', 'Sentimental Blue'; *Silene* 'Swan Lake'; *Myosotis* 'Victoria Rose', 'Victoria Blue'.

Group I growing strategy. Cool plugs for four weeks in a cooler (35°F); place under natural days. Natural days may persist for the entire crop, or if lights are already available, you can switch plants to long days after four to five weeks. If plugs are transplanted without cooling to finished container, grow in a cool greenhouse (35 to 45°F) under natural days until four to six weeks prior to market, then raise temperatures accordingly.

Group II: Quantitative long-day plants. Long days accelerate flowering, but plants will flower under short days as well. They include: *Aquilegia* x *hybrida* 'Song Bird' series (benefit of cold questionable); *Anchusa capensis* 'Blue Bedder'; *Anemone sylvestris; Cerastium tomentosum* (for flowers only, should be grown under natural days for foliage plant); *Chrysanthemum* x *superbum; Coreopsis* 'Early Sunrise'; *Gaillardia pulchella* 'Goblin'; *Gypsophila repens; Oenothera tetragona; Phlox subulata; Scabiosa* 'Butterfly Blue'; *Salvia* x *superba* 'Blue Queen', 'Lubeca'; *Veronica* 'Blue Bouquet'.

Group II growing strategy. Cool plugs for no more than eight weeks in a cooler; longer times may be used in the greenhouse. After removing plants from the cooler, place them under natural days for four to six weeks for vegetative growth and compact habit, then move to long days if available. If long days are not available, plants will be two to four weeks later.

Group III: Qualitative long-day plants. Long days are required. Plants won't flower in a reasonable time under short days. They include: *Asclepias tuberosa; Campanula carpatica* 'Clips'; *Catananche caerulea; Coreopsis verticillata* 'Moonbeam'; *Echinacea purpurea* 'Bravado', 'White Swan'.

Group III growing strategy. Cool plugs in a cooler for four to eight weeks to reduce bench time. Place under natural days for four to six weeks, then transfer to long days four to eight weeks before flowering. If long days aren't available, find some lights. Plants may also be cooled on benches.

Group IV: Plants in which cooling is necessary. Plants won't flower in a reasonable time without significant cooling. This is a difficult category because the plug size may have a large influence. They include: *Arabis sturii, Achillea millefolium, Aster alpinus, Coreopsis grandiflora* 'Sunray', *Gypsophila repens, Gypsophila* 'Pierre's Pink', *Cerastium tomentosum.*

Group IV growing strategy. Cool plugs for at least eight weeks, place under the appropriate photoperiod.

Group V. Plants that don't fit into the previous five groupings. This may end up containing quite a few. They include: *Cerastium tomentosum* (for flowers, Group V; for foliage, short days only), *Saxifraga arendsii* 'Purple Robe' (short day/long day plant, that is, short days must occur before long days for flowering).

July 1996

To-the-Day Perennial Timing

"Growers are beginning to ask for exact recipes for blooming perennials on a specific date," perennial grower Todd Swift, Swift Greenhouses Inc., Gilman, Iowa, told GrowerExpo attendees in his presentation, Growing Perennials from Plugs. Here's an excerpt from his presentation:

Key perennial dates to remember begin in late May to late June, when you should sow your 288 plug trays or begin taking cuttings, sticking them directly into 50 plug trays. Grow seed items on for eight to ten weeks from late June to August, when you transplant them into 50-cell trays. From mid-September to mid-November, grow on 50-cell trays and count nodes to ensure maturity. Vernalization should occur from mid-November to February. Then, transplant the dormant 50s into 4½-in. pots in February. Force and grow on the 4½-in. plants at 60°F, lighting the long-day plants as necessary until April, when plants will be ready for sale.

Approximate Node Number	Species/ Variety	Plug Size	Average No. of Days to Flower	Response to Long Days	Cold Treatment	Weeks of Cold Chamber
15	Aquilegia	50	60	No response (most varieties)	Required (most varieties)	10 or more
—	Coreopsis 'Moonbeam'	Bare root	39	Required	Beneficial	15
12	Gaillardia grandiflora	32	48	Beneficial	Required	10
16	Heuchera sanguinea	288	37	No response	Required	10
40+ leaves	Iberis	50	22	No response	Required	10
20 to 25+	Lavender	50 128	47 52	Required	Required	15
—	Leucanthemum 'Snow Lady'	50	45	Required	Beneficial	10
10	Rudbeckia 'Goldsturm'	Bare root	81	Required	Recommended	10
4 to 5	Salvia 'Blue Queen'	128	31	Required	Required	10 to 15
<4 to 5	Veronica 'SunnyBorder Blue'	50	64	No response	Required	10

*Chart based on transplanting into 4½-in. pots.

In addition, Todd, with the help of Michigan State University, put together a chart for quick reference on targeting your perennials' flowering. Here are guidelines for the top ten perennials he produces. Use them to develop your own formulas for success.

May 1999

Going Commercial with Forced Perennials

Chris Beytes

A few years ago, Post Gardens didn't even grow perennials. In 1995, as owner Jerry Tuinier describes it, the Michigan business "played" with a small number of assorted perennials just to see what they were all about.

Last year, they "jumped in feet first," expanding perennial production by a whopping 2,000%. This year they've doubled production, and Jerry forecasts similar increases down the road. A few other growers have reported similar phenomenal growth in perennials.

What's behind this amazing expansion? The answer is forcing research, courtesy of Michigan State University (MSU), the University of Georgia, and others that for the first time lets you grown and bloom perennials on *your* schedule, not the plants'. Growers such as Post Gardens are putting the detailed research of MSU's Drs. Royal Heins and Art Cameron to work commercially, with obvious success.

Improving on Nature

That perennials are experiencing a resurgent popularity with gardeners is a given. But perennials have their limitations. Most only bloom for a short time once a year. And many have wild, unkempt habits that make them less than appealing for retail sale in a pot and useless as a houseplant. The goals of the forcing research are straightforward: find out what it takes to grow various perennials that have tight, compact, well-shaped habits and find out how to make them bloom on a precise schedule any time of year.

University research has solved these problems, giving growers a wider selection of blooming plants to sell for more months of the year. Some perennials, such as *Campanula,* can even be sold year-round as pot plants. Many perennials will last indoors for several weeks before being planted outside. Forced perennials are also beginning to be accepted by mass merchandisers who want to compete against traditional perennial specialists.

While MSU's cookbook-style forcing instructions have been well documented in *GrowerTalks* and other trade journals, little is known about how the research works in commercial greenhouses. Just as important is how consumers respond to out-of-season perennials. While a handful of growers are experimenting with the forcing research, few have gone into it as quickly and as thoroughly as Post Gardens.

Perennials as Bedding?

Post Gardens, with locations in Battle Creek and Rockwood, isn't a long-time perennial grower that has adapted forcing techniques to its standard perennial production. As mentioned above, Post Gardens didn't even grow perennials until 1995. Jerry says Post Gardens had been a long-time supporter of MSU research and agreed to help finance perennial research three years ago. MSU researchers told Jerry he was "missing the boat" by not growing perennials, so two years ago Post Gardens brought in about 10,000 assorted plants for research and development. While Jerry didn't use any forcing research on these first plants, he recognized the potential, and Post Gardens made a full-fledged entry into forced perennials in 1996.

Forcing perennials isn't like growing bedding plants, Jerry stresses. In fact, critics of the perennial forcing concept worry that the new techniques will essentially turn perennials into bedding plants, destroying their image as a high-end floriculture item. Jerry doesn't buy that. He says that bedding plants are much easier to grow, requiring few, if any, special techniques such as lighting, blackclothing, and cooling. Also, he says, "Perennials won't take over any other markets like bedding plants because people use [perennials] as highlight plants, more like shrubbery." Bedding is more often used for splashes of color at the front of beds.

Doing What MSU Says

Following and sticking to the strict cultural requirements MSU has outlined is the most important part of successfully forcing perennials. Jerry says, "There's a lot more science to it than with any other crop." Published articles on the topic are fine, he adds, but it still takes a one-on-one relationship with MSU's researchers to succeed.

Financially supporting MSU's research has given Post Gardens and other growers an inside look at the university's research results, with the added benefit of hands-on assistance from Art and Royal, who answer questions and make visits to businesses. Jerry describes a horror story from one grower who suffered the loss of about 100,000 perennials because he didn't follow MSU's recommendations to the letter. But, "if you do *precisely* what they say," Jerry emphasizes, "it's going to work."

"Doing what they say" means having the ability to light, blackcloth, and cool your perennials. Post Gardens built one acre of Cravo retractable-roof greenhouses (Jerry says a retractable roof isn't necessary, but you *must* have 100% control of your greenhouse environment) and installed lights and a blackcloth system. Lights can be simple incandescent fixtures such as those used for mum and poinsettia lighting. Post Gardens also has a cooler for vernalizing perennials.

It's the precise combination of these cultural factors, chemical growth regulators, and proper water and nutrition that influence the habit and bloom time of perennials. For instance, Jerry says certain plants may require twelve hours of light, then five hours of darkness, then a certain amount of light again. A two-minute deviation from this precise schedule could keep the crop from blooming. Another crop may require long days for six weeks, short days for another six weeks, or vice versa. Being able to accurately and easily control all of these factors is the key to success, as is carefully following MSU's recommendations.

Jerry won't reveal the exact crop mix he's forcing, but it's safe to assume he's trying all of the crops that MSU has published information on, such as *Campanula, Rudbeckia,* and *Coreopsis,* along with the new ones they're keeping under wraps. He'll add varieties as information comes available. All perennials are grown in 6-in. pots and are sold as a mix, but Jerry says he'll grow specific varieties for customers if they give him enough notice.

Last year, Post Gardens started selling blooming perennials in April and didn't finish up until October. Eventually, Jerry expects to have perennials available almost year-round. And with forcing, he can have fall perennials available for spring and vice versa.

Retail Interest Is Growing

Post Gardens sells forced perennials to mass market outlets, garden center chains and independent retailers, but it's the chains that are moving big volumes. Jerry says while his chain customers are "very interested" in the idea of year-round perennials and are increasing their orders ever year, they haven't stopped carrying traditional perennials. In fact, about 50% of what Post Gardens sells isn't forced. Instead, half of their sales are "staple items"—traditional top-selling perennials such as hostas, which don't require any special growing techniques.

Their investment in MSU's research program is the main reason Jerry cites for Post Garden's leap into forced perennials. "It's an exciting crop for us," he says, adding that bedding plant sales haven't been increasing. "We were getting stale, growing the same old stuff." Jerry and his customers benefit from increased sales due to perennials' popularity and novelty and from a longer sales season. Consumers benefit by seeing the plants in bloom rather than buying them green and relying on a tag or sign to tell them what they're getting.

What about the argument that customers will be confused by a plant that's blooming in May when it will naturally bloom in August the next season? Jerry doesn't see that as a problem. First, tags and signs explain the natural bloom period of the plant. Second, a plant forced to bloom early should bloom again at its natural time, giving customers more for their money.

Forced Perennials Here to Stay

Just how important will forced perennials be for our industry? Very, if Post Gardens' enthusiasm and success are a clue. In fact, Jerry asked that specific numbers, varieties, and cultural techniques be kept "off the record"—after all, he's invested heavily in both MSU's research program and his own business expansion to capitalize on this growing market. Naturally, he wants to maintain his competitive advantage as long as he can.

Perennial Research: Where's It Headed?

"Part of the fun and the frustration [of perennial research] is that there are so many of the darn things," says Dr. Art Cameron, MSU, Lansing. Art, along with Dr. Royal Heins and a team of assistants, has led the field in perennial forcing research. While the MSU researchers have developed "cookbook" instructions for forcing some of the most economically important perennials, their work is far from over. Art stresses that MSU is still very active in perennial forcing research and has significant funding still coming into the program.

MSU research covers an extremely broad base of categories, including vernalization, photoperiod, and scheduling. Their latest focus is on propagation, for example, using photoperiod to manipulate stock plant growth. Art says short and long days can have a major effect on how well stock plants produce cuttings and on how well those cuttings root. With growers producing so many perennials vegetatively, this research could be important for helping propagators increase production.

While research at universities and commercial greenhouses has given us a wealth of data about how light, temperature, day length, juvenility, and other factors affect perennials, we still have a long way to go before we can grow a coreopsis as consistently year-round as a chrysanthemum.

Says Dr. Allan Armitage, University of Georgia, Athens, another leader in perennial research: "A major question is still the scheduling—

making sure you can get [perennials] to do what you want, when you want it." He explains that while some perennials, such as Shasta daisies, are fairly easy to bloom any time of year, other crops just don't want to bloom out of their natural season.

Much of the problem lies in the lack of consistency among perennials in general. Little breeding work has been done—most varieties come about through natural selection. Also, seed lots vary widely. Very few F_1 hybrid perennials are on the market.

Jelitto and Benary are among the breeding companies that have introduced a few improved perennial varieties. Allan mentions a new columbine from Benary that could be "a real nice forceable item." But overall, perennials are a long way away from having the consistency of bedding plants. And while Allan and others have focused heavily on new and unusual varieties both in annuals and perennials, "they're never going to be big value items," he says. Plus, many of these unusual varieties are vegetatively propagated, making them more expensive than seed-propagated plants.

To help solve the problem of variety improvement, Drs. John Erwin, Peter Ascher, and Mark Strefeler of the University of Minnesota, St. Paul, have focused their new research program specifically on perennial breeding and crop physiology. Mark reports that they're currently evaluating which perennial species to work with, based on commercial importance and potential for improvement. A few crops he says that show potential are *Sedum, Aster, Euphorbia, Asclepias,* and perennial *Verbena.*

Improvements could include plant habit, flower color and form, and pest and disease resistance (for instance, *Phlox,* notoriously susceptible to powdery mildew, could benefit from crosses with existing mildew-resistant species). The researchers plan to use the latest in genetic engineering technology, including tissue culture and gene transfer. Gene gun technology could be especially useful for developing new colors of standard perennials, Mark says.

While commercial production capability is important and will be part of Minnesota's breeding program, researchers will also focus heavily on garden performance, especially for the state's harsh climate. This summer they'll be trialing about 215 different varieties from 15 genera in a Minneapolis park to begin evaluating their suitability for the research program. They've also been talking with growers to find out their needs, and they welcome input from the industry.

Unfortunately, perennial breeding is a long, slow process. The relative lack of perennial breeding work by the large commercial bedding and pot plant breeders illustrates this. But thanks to the universities, we've learned more about perennials in the last five years than in the last twenty-five. More groundbreaking discoveries may be just around the corner.

June 1997

Forcing at Ivy Acres

Chris Beytes

While a few growers such as Post Gardens (see article "Going Commercial with Forced Perennials" above) are striving to force perennials nearly year-round, New York's Ivy Acres is using forcing techniques to extend their season and to increase quality.

"We use [forcing] to get an early season jump," says Sara Mitchell-Stika, Ivy Acres' marketing manager, blooming spring crops such as *Gaillardia* and *Coreopsis* for sale in late March and April. When spring hits, Ivy Acres concentrates on its core crop: bedding plants. According to Sara, perennials aren't as profitable as bedding plants for spring because they can't be turned as quickly. For late-season sales, Ivy Acres uses forcing techniques not to bring plants into bloom early, but to increase uniformity of bloom.

Sara says Ivy Acres has been working with Allan Armitage for six or seven years, so they have considerable experience with forcing. They've also been a strong supporter of Michigan State University research. But still, "it's a tricky thing," she says. "The book may be written, but there are a lot of factors we don't know yet."

June 1997

Juvenility: Your Perennial Crop's Age Affects Flowering

Art Cameron, Mei Yuan, Royal Heins, and Will Carlson

The last few years at Michigan State University we've studied flowering requirements for a wide range of herbaceous perennials whose flowering usually is regulated by two primary environmental factors: cold and photoperiod. We've established protocols for flowering perennials originally grown from seed in plug trays. In many cases, seedlings can be chilled in plug trays, transplanted and forced directly into flower either under natural days or long days, depending on the particular species requirements. However, we've encountered a number of instances in which seedlings wouldn't flower even after a significant period of cold followed by exposure to long days (after ten weeks of cold, columbines didn't bloom, regardless of plus size [128 or 50] or photoperiod) (figure 1). In addition, poppy, statice, Alpine aster and columbine seedlings rarely bloomed, regardless of the treatments we used.

In one experiment, we tested the flowering response of coral bells (*Heuchera sanguinea*). To determine the effect of plant size, we used seedlings from 128- and 50-cell trays. None of the coral bells flowered when transferred directly to the greenhouse for forcing without a cold treatment (figure 2). A second group of coral bells was chilled for ten weeks, then forced under short days (nine hours) or long days (nine hours of light plus a four-hour night interruption from 10:00 till 2:00 using 20 f.c. of incandescent lighting). No plants from the 128-cell trays flowered, while plants from the 50-cell trays bloomed after cold, regardless of photoperiodic treatment. (Coral bells are day-neutral.)

Juvenility—A Matter of Age

Why didn't any of the columbines flower and only the 50-cell-sized coral bells flower in these experiments? It's a matter of age. Some plants were just too young to flower, even when provided with normally inductive conditions. Plant physiologists refer to these plants as juvenile. Coral bells seedlings from the 128-cell trays were apparently below the threshold age (juvenile), while those from 50-cell trays were above it (mature). This doesn't imply that all coral bells from 50-cell trays will flower, and it does not imply that all seedlings of different species from 50-cell trays will flower. It simply means that the seedlings from 50-cell trays were old enough to flower.

The juvenility period usually refers to early phases of growth when plants won't flower even if exposed to favorable conditions. The duration of the juvenile period in flowering plants varies widely. In many woody plants, it isn't uncommon for it to last several years. Notable

Figure 1. Columbine plants have a lengthy juvenile period. Plants didn't flower even after ten weeks cold because they were still juvenile. "Small" seedlings (left) were produced in 128-cell trays and had an average of seven leaves, while "large" seedlings (right) were produced in 50-cell trays and had an average of eleven leaves.

examples include apples and other fruit crops. In fact, the juvenile phase can last twenty to thirty years in some forest trees.

In contrast, the juvenile period for most herbaceous perennials we've studied is less than one year and can usually be measured in weeks or months. Some exceptions include bulb crops, which can take two to three seasons to begin flowering.

Determining Age—A Practical Approach

One thing is for certain: You can't tell the age of a herbaceous perennial simply by the size of the plug tray in which it is produced. Also, seedling age doesn't take into account the temperature or photoperiod under which seedlings are grown.

Different growers may use different methods of production, and these can influence the physiological age of seedlings. In fact, in different-sized plug trays we've received plants that were very similar in size, age, and response to treatments.

In practice, one method of determining seedling age is to count the number of leaves or nodes that have been produced. Leaf counts have long been used to measure age in tracking the development of plants such as poinsettia and Easter lily. Leaf counts inherently include temperature effects: Plants grow faster at higher temperatures and produce more leaves.

Growers have little information about the number of leaves needed for various herbaceous perennials to become mature. Table 1 includes information from two to three years of trials on the critical leaf number for perennials. Most of these plants have an obligate cold requirement. For some plants listed, we simply know that plants of a given age didn't flower in our experiments.

For a few of these perennials, we've conducted rather extensive trials to determine critical leaf number. For instance, we further examined the juvenility-period requirement for coral bells. Only plants with about

Table 1. Age Requirements for Flowering of a Number of Common Herbaceous Perennials (In some cases, the specific minimum age has not been determined.)

Plant name	Common name	Age requirements
Achillea filipendulina 'Cloth of Gold'	Yarrow	Plants with eight to thirteen leaves flowered inconsistently.
Aquilegia—most species	Columbine	Extended juvenile period—for some species at least fifteen leaves are required for consistent bloom.
Aster alpinus	Alpine aster	Plants require at least fifteen leaves to flower consistently.
Astilbe arendsii	Astilbe	Plants with five to six leaves flowered very inconsistently.
Chrysanthemum coccineum	Pyrethrum	Plants require at least fifteen leaves to flower consistently.
Coreopsis 'Sunray'	Tickseed	Juvenile phase ends with about sixteen leaves.
Delphinium grandiflorum	Delphinium	Plants with four to five leaves flower.
Echinacea purpurea	Coneflower	Plants with four leaves flower.
Euphorbia epithymoides	Cushion spurge	Plants with six to eight leaves failed to flower.
Goniolimon tataricum	Statice	Plants with ten to fourteen leaves failed to flower.
Heuchera sanguinea	Coral bells	Plants require sixteen leaves to flower consistently.
Kniphofia uvaria	Red hot poker	Field-grown plants failed to flower-presumably a two-year juvenile period.
Lavandula angustifolia	Lavender	Most consistent flowering with forty to fifty leaves.
Lobelia 'Compliment Scarlet'	Cardinal flower	Plants with six to seven leaves will flower.
Papaver orientale 'Brilliant'	Oriental poppy	Plants with ten to fourteen leaves failed to flower.
Physostegia virginiana	Obedience plant	Plants require at least ten leaves to flower consistently.
Rudbeckia fulgida 'Goldsturm'	Black-eyed Susan	Juvenile phase ends at about ten leaves.
Veronica spicata 'Blue'	Speedwell	Plants with six to eight leaves will flower.

sixteen leaves flowered 100%. Note that seedlings from 128-cell trays, shown in figure 1, had an average of seven leaves, while those from 50-cell trays had about fourteen leaves. Thus, by coincidence, plants we initially tested were just over (128-cell trays) and below (50-cell trays) the threshold number.

Figure 2. Only the "large" plug-grown seedlings of coral bells flowered and then only after ten weeks of cold treatment. 2A (left) "Small" seedlings were produced in 128-cell trays and had an average of seven leaves, while 2B (right) "large" seedlings were produced in 50-cell trays and had an average of fourteen leaves.

If you want to get a general idea of a seedling population's age, it's best to count a random group of many individual seedlings and take the average. Also, count only leaves of single plants. Perennial producers will often seed two, three or even more seeds per cell, and it could be misleading to count all of these seedlings and assume the total is that of a single plant. In addition, counting leaves can be difficult after plants have received cold treatment because of senescence and winter burn. Still, leaf counts are simple to perform and are generally a reliable means of estimating plant age.

Not all herbaceous perennials have an extended juvenility period. Some, such as Carpathian harebells (*Campanula carpatica*), will flower in the plug trays if given long-day photoperiods. Others flower readily regardless of starting material age. However, for those perennials with a definite juvenility period, it's important that they reach minimum leaf counts before the beginning of the cold period. In many cases, this can be accomplished by growing plants under twelve- to thirteen-hour photoperiods for several weeks before initiating cold treatment, ensuring more uniform flowering on larger plants.

Chapter 5
Pest and Disease Control

Pest Control on Perennials

Mary Harris

Perennial plants can harbor perennial pests. Unless you're reducing production time by buying vernalized plugs to produce sale-ready perennials, you may encounter some unexpected pest problems on plants being started this summer for sale next spring.

Sanitation

Remove leaf litter and debris from plants to be winterized. Several pests overwinter underneath such discarded material. Use a clean mulch instead of leaf litter if you need a layer for root protection. Weeds also provide winter refuge for insects, and the long cropping time required to produce marketable perennials also increases the need for weed control. Preemergence herbicides can be used on many perennials without phytotoxicity. These products are formulated to remain near the soil surface where weed seeds germinate and not to penetrate deeper where they could affect established roots.

Commitment to Scouting

Early detection is essential for insect control on perennials. Monitoring provides the information needed to make good treatment decisions. Choose a reliable employee, and devote that person's time to scouting. A good scout should be trained to recognize and distinguish different pests and should know which monitoring methods are appropriate for each pest. Training is an investment that will pay off. A trained scout should *regularly* monitor pests throughout all growing areas. This takes a commitment by you to allow your scout to do the job and not to pull that person off scouting for other tasks that are "more important."

Early detection and response will reduce overall control costs. Pests detected early can be suppressed by spot treatments. Treating only infested plants saves on chemical costs and reduces pest exposure, which also reduces the development of insecticide resistance.

Whiteflies

Whiteflies are the No. 1 insect pest in perennial production. Some plants that support heavy infestations include *Lantana, Verbena, Veronica, Echinacea, Rudbeckia,* and *Salvia.* The most effective control program should begin with an application of Marathon when the plant begins to put on foliage in the spring. This should provide protection for several weeks to two months. Continue scouting plants using yellow sticky cards, one per 10,000 sq. ft., to count adults. Also examine the undersides of leaves to detect immature whiteflies. If additional control action becomes necessary, don't reapply Marathon. Instead, treat with a tank mix of a pyrethroid such as Mavrik and a soap such as M-Pede. Alternate with treatments of an Orthene/M-Pede mix. Always continue monitoring to determine the efficacy of your treatments and the need for further action.

Aphids

Aphids can appear and build up rapidly on several plants such as *Verbena* and daylilies. Aphid infestations should be detected as early as possible by inspecting foliage—and using sticky cards isn't sufficient. Look for aphids on stems and the undersides of leaves. When an infestation is detected, it should be spot treated. Marathon provides good aphid control, but it may not be cost effective if used only for this pest. A combination of Orthene and any insecticidal oil such as Sunspray Ultrafine or Saf-T-Side is a good treatment for a moderate aphid infestation. To reduce heavy infestations, Thiodan or nicotine can be effective. Subsequent treatments of insecticidal soaps or oils can then be used along with continuous monitoring.

Leafminers

Leafminers can quickly damage the foliage of columbine, dahlia, larkspur, and salvia. Yellow sticky cards are good tools for detecting the presence of leafminers before they cause noticeable damage. Citation is now registered for leafminers in greenhouse and container-grown ornamentals, as is Avid. Both insecticides are applied to the foliage at seven-day intervals.

Spider Mites

Spider mites are another perennial pest. Infestations may not occur each year but can be heavy on columbine, daylilies, Shasta daisy, *Platycodon,* and salvia. Foliage inspection is necessary to detect spider mites at low population levels. After treatment application, you must continue monitoring to determine if the miticides you are using are doing the job because resistance is often encountered when trying to control mites. A pyrethroid such as Tame can be used for quick knockdown. Pentac is slower acting but still provides good control in the greenhouse. If the mite population doesn't decrease following an application, it's very likely a resistant strain and you need to rotate chemicals to determine what works.

It's always advisable to test a few plants first for phytotoxicity before applying any untried pesticide to an entire crop.

April 1996

Insect Pests of Perennials

Joanne Lutz

With the wide array of perennials grown today, it's critical to come up with control strategies before extensive damage occurs. Crucial keys for pest managers include early detection, knowledge of key pests, and distinguishing symptoms from the damage produced by an insect's mouthpart. Time of year, location on a plant, and thresholds are other key factors influencing control options. Insects can be classified by mouthpart (either chewing or piercing-sucking) and can either feed internally between the leaf tissue or bore into stems and crowns.

Chewing Insects

Chewing insects such as caterpillars and sawflies can cause extensive damage when feeding on leaf surfaces. Look for frass (debris or excrement produced by insects); turn leaves over and inspect carefully. Perennials that are frequently damaged by caterpillars and should be monitored closely include: *Artemisia* 'Silver Brocade', *Polygonum, Heuchera* 'Autumn Bride', *Monarda, Hemerocallis, Pulmonaria, Primula,* and *Asclepias.* Also, carefully monitor hibiscus and ferns for sawflies. Horticultural oils, insecticidal soap, and *Bacillus thuringiensis* (DiPel) can be used on eggs and early-instar caterpillars. *Beauveria bassiana* (Naturalis-O), neem pesticides (azadirachtin), or insect growth regulators such as diflubenzuron (Adept) are good biorational pesticides to use in the greenhouse on larvae. Pyrethrums have quick knockdowns and short residuals, while synthetic pyrethroids such as Talstar or Decathalon have longer residuals, work on contact, and are broad-spectrum pesticides. Adults are only controlled if they ingest or come in contact with the pesticide residue.

Japanese or Oriental beetles, black vine weevils, and grasshoppers cause damage such as leaf chewing, leaf notching, or skeletonizing leaves and flowers. Beetles are attracted to *Aster, Astilbe, Gaillardia, Hibiscus, Oenothera, Rudbeckia, Polygonatum* (silver lace vine), and *Phlox.* Black vine weevils at nursery operations can cause significant damage and will become a serious pest if left unchecked. Adults are difficult to find, but the damage they leave behind isn't. They feed at night on outer leaf margins and leave a notching pattern that can reduce perennials' aesthetic quality. However, it's the larvae that can cause significant damage—not by feeding on leaves, but on roots. *Astible, Bergenia, Sedum, Tricyrtis, Polygonum, Rodgersia, Filipendula, Helleborus, Hosta,* and *Liriope* seem to be some of the weevils' favorites. The beneficial nematode *Heterorhabditis bacteriophora* (such as the cruiser nematode) is an excellent biological pesticide and should be applied when soil temperatures are between 60 to 90°F. Marathon (imidacloprid) granules, Orthene, or Turcam at label intervals can reduce adult feeding.

Slugs and snails can cause irregular chewed holes in leaves and deposit unsightly slime trails. These night feeders can defoliate and destroy tender young seedlings. During the day, they can be found under pots and flats. Slugs favor *Belamcanda, Tradescantia, Aster,* and *Iris cristata,* while snails prefer *Achillea, Campanula, Viola, Delphinium, Hemerocallis, Hosta, Gypsophila, Dianthus, Papaver,* and *Saponaria.* Control is best achieved by reducing conditions that attract moisture: Provide wider spacing to allow for good air circulation, and monitor watering practices that allow foliage to be dry by evening. Products such as diatomaceous earth or slug baits are effective if applied at label intervals.

Leafhoppers can cause twisted foliage, chlorotic leaves, and discolored or deformed flowers. Look on leaf undersides for nymphs or adults and their shed skins. Perennials that leafhoppers find attractive include *Aster, Oenothera, Tanacetum, Centaurea, Coreopsis, Phlox, Rudbeckia, Wisteria, Gypsophila, Gaura,* and *Helianthemum.* Repeated applications of insecticidal soap and insect growth regulators or systemic pesticides are necessary because of the need to control multiple generations.

Boring Insects

Boring insects cause damage when larvae enter stems or other plant parts and feed inside, causing decline, dieback, or death. The European corn borer and stalk borer are the two most common, although many species of beetles are also known as borers. Monitor *Aster, Chrysanthemum, Delphinium, Gaillardia, Dianthus, Phlox, Rudbeckia, Persicaria, Lychnis,* and *Salvia*. Removing infected stems and sanitizing in fall will help reduce overwintering. Chemical pesticides generally aren't effective once the borers are inside the stems.

Leafminers are mining insects whose larvae feed within the leaves of plants, causing light green or white serpentine trails that turn brown. Larvae eventually emerge from the leaf; however, the damage is already done. Susceptible perennial plants include *Aquilegia, Senecio, Chrysanthemum, Salvia, Veronica, Delphinium, Gypsophila,* and *Aconitum.*

Piercing-Sucking Insects

The piercing-sucking group includes thrips, aphids, whitefly, and mites. They have sharp, needlelike mouthparts that pierce plant cells and draw the sap, leaving signs of small specks, chlorotic spots or streaking, often with some twisted, stunted, or curled growth. Often, a toxic reaction occurs from the saliva of some insects, which can be damaging to the perennial.

Thrips can be the most economically destructive pest because of the known transmission of the plant-damaging tospoviruses INSV and TSWV from at least three thrips species. The western flower thrips is the most prevalent species found throughout the U.S. The larvae feed on an infected plant and then transmit the virus to other plants through feeding. Look for tiny black fecal spots and silvery streaking of foliage (caused by the rasping-sucking mouthpart) when monitoring. Perennials to scout for thrips damage include *Papaver, Lupinus, Hemerocallis, Platycodon, Phlox, Verbena, Geranium, Asclepias, Tradescantia,* and *Alcea*. Herbaceous perennials found with the tospovirus include *Lobelia, Stokesia, Hosta, Tricyrtis, Helleborus, Physostegia,* and *Polemonium*. Biological controls of thrips include predatory phytoseiid mites, minute pirate bug (*Orius* spp.) and the entomopathogenic fungus *Beauveria bassiana*. Chemical pesticide choices for control include Conserve, Azatin XL, Decathlon, Orthene, DuraGuard, or Talstar. Multiple applications five days apart are often necessary for control.

Aphids are frustrating pests due to their high reproduction rate and resistance to most pesticides. Green peach aphid, melon aphid, chrysanthemum aphid, and foxglove aphid are the most common, although many other species are found on perennials and grasses. Good indicators of damage include twisted, stunted new growth and the presence of shed skin and honeydew, as aphids also serve as vectors of viruses. Aphid perennial favorites include *Achillea, Aquilegia, Chrysanthemum, Digitalis, Dianthus, Viola, Sedum, Oenothera, Monarda, Alcea, Ajuga, Salvia,* and *Hypericum*. Effective biological control choices include ladybird beetles, green lacewings, aphid midges, parasitic wasps, and *Beauveria bassiana*. Biorational pesticides include insecticidal soaps, horticultural oils, and insect growth regulators.

Common mite pests include the two-spotted spider mite, cyclamen mite, and broad mite. Fine webbing, stippled foliage, and yellow or bronze leaves are indicators of activity of the two-spotted spider mite. Perennials mites find attractive include *Buddleia, Scabiosa, Knautia, Salvia, Lobelia, Caryopteris, Verbena, Geum, Alcea, Viola, Asclepias,* and *Crocosmia*. Miticides for two-spotted spider mites include Sanmite, Hexygon, Avid, Floramite, and Cinnamite. Horticultural oils can be used as a control. Although they're invisible to the naked eye, cyclamen and broad mites' damage is identified by twisted, curled, brittle, darkened, or scabby new growth. *Stachys, Delphinium, Aconitum, Verbena, Clematis, Viola,* and *Chrysanthemum* are favorites of this mite. Cyclamen and broad mites require repeat applications of Kelthane, Talstar, or Thiodan.

Whiteflies are generally greenhouse pests but can become a nuisance outdoors on host plants. The most common species include greenhouse whitefly, silverleaf whitefly, and the bandedwinged whitefly. Yellowing, reduced vigor, or tiny, white flying insects when plants are disturbed are key symptoms of whitefly. Honeydew and sooty mold are also associated with whitefly populations. Perennials whiteflies find attractive are *Hibiscus, Eupatorium, Veronica, Salvia, Nepeta, Rudbeckia, Vernonia, Alcea, Boltonia, Aster,* and *Verbena*. Biological control includes *Beauveria bassiana* and *Encarsia formosa*. Horticultural oils, insecticidal soaps, or insect growth regulators work well when thoroughly applied to lower leaf surfaces. Many chemical pesticides are labeled for whitefly control, including Tame, Orthene, Topcide and Resmethrin.

Good sanitation, inspection, and quarantine of incoming plants will help reduce the introduction of unwanted insects into your greenhouse and nursery. Before applying controls, know the key pests and the appropriate pesticides to apply at the most vulnerable stage of the life cycle. Avoid stressful conditions, and follow a nutrient management program to provide optimum growing conditions to give your plants a better chance to tolerate insect attack.

June 1999

Perennial Disease Watch

Cheryl Smith

Now is the time your perennials are at risk for disease infestation, but knowing what to watch for is half the battle. Here we've put together a quick guide to common diseases. To prevent disease resistance when using fungicides, rotate products from different chemical families.

Botrytis Blight

Common hosts: *Aster, Rudbeckia, Paeonia, Salvia.*

Monitoring: Wounded, older, and young succulent tissues are particularly susceptible. May cause leaf spots, leaf blights, stem cankers, and cutting rots. Under high humidity, a fuzzy gray, gray-green or gray-brown "mold" may develop.

Management: Sanitize; remove and destroy infected tissues. Increase plant spacing for air circulation; remove older plant parts; deadhead plants; remove all crop debris; avoid overfertilization with nitrogen; vent and heat at dusk to reduce humidity.

Root and Stem Rots

Common hosts: All are susceptible.

Monitoring: Symptoms resembles those of nutrient deficiency, usually on older foliage first. Wilting, stunting. Media in containers may remain wet for long periods after watering.

Pythium: Infected roots are grayish brown and appear water-soaked; root cortex easily pulls off when plant is pulled from soil; black stem. Favored by cool, wet soils; poor drainage; and soluble salts injury.

Rhizoctonia: Stems shrivel and turn brown at soil line. High humidity and warm temperatures favor infection.

Sclerotinia: Causes tan, brown or straw-colored stem cankers; black, hard masses of fungal growth called sclerotia (resemble rodent droppings) often form in pith or on stem. Under high humidity, cottony white growth may appear on lower stem.

Sclerotium: Similar to *Sclerotinia*, but stems may become shredded. Sclerotia are small, brown, and resemble mustard seeds.

Management: Avoid overwatering or splashing soil when watering. Water early in day; keep water nozzles off ground. Remove and destroy symptomatic plants; test soluble salts levels regularly; and space plants to improve air circulation.

Powdery Mildew

Common hosts: *Aquilegia, Lupinus, Monarda, Phlox,* many others.

Monitoring: Powdery white, grayish white or brownish white growth on upper and lower leaf surfaces or stems. Doesn't require free moisture on leaves to germinate and infect. Prolonged periods of high humidity and warm temperatures (above 70°F) favor development.

Management: Improve air circulation; use resistant cultivars.

Leaf Spots and Blights

Common hosts: *Aquilegia, Aster, Bergenia, Chrysanthemum, Coreopsis, Delphinium, Hosta, Iris, Liatris, Monarda, Rudbeckia, Veronica.*

Monitoring: Spots are discolored or dead areas on foliage or blossoms; blights result when spots coalesce or when large tissue areas are infected. May be spread through handling, through cuttings, and in seed. Splashing water spreads bacteria.

Management: Follow same procedures as for *Botrytis*. Avoid overhead watering and splashing water.

Viral Diseases

The most common viruses that cause diseases on perennials are: cucumber mosaic virus (CMV), tobacco mosaic virus (TMV), impatiens necrotic spot virus (INSV), tomato spotted wilt virus (TSWV), poty viruses (POTY) and alfalfa mosaic virus (AMV).

Monitoring: Black or brown spots on foliage; mosaic; stunting; black, brown or chlorotic ring spots on foliage or stems; chlorotic or yellow oak-leaf pattern on leaves. Primary insect vectors are aphids and thrips (most commonly western flower thrips). Many viruses are also sap-transmitted: CMV, AMV and POTY (aphids); TMV (people); INSV and TSWV (thrips).

Management: Inspect incoming plant material. Isolate suspect plants until diagnosis is confirmed. Destroy infected plants. Don't hold plant material year to year. Monitor insect populations. Grow resistant cultivars or virus-indexed material.

Rust Diseases

Common hosts: *Aconitum, Anemone, Aquilegia, Delphinium, Liatris, Monarda, Potentilla.*

Monitoring: Pale yellow or light green spots or pustules on upper leaf surfaces; powdery pustules on lower leaf surfaces (below chlorotic spots on upper leaf surfaces) or on petioles and stems. Pustules may be filled with rusty brown, yellow, cream, orange, white, or black spores.

Management: Water early in day; remove infected plants, bagging material to prevent spore dispersal.

Downy Mildew

Common hosts: *Aster, Artemesia, Centaurea, Geranium, Geum, Lupinus, Rudbeckia, Veronica.*

Monitoring: Pale, yellow patches on upper leaf surfaces; older, infected areas may be browned; plants may be stunted. Under high humidity, undersides of yellow patches are covered with a dense, whitish, tan, gray or violet/beige fungal growth. Older leaves are infected first. Can be seed-borne.

Management: Remove and destroy infected plants as soon as possible; remove all crop debris at end of season; remove related weed hosts; water early in day to promote drying before nightfall.

June 1999

Managing Weeds in Perennials

Joseph C. Neal

When it comes to weeds, "Start clean, stay clean" should be every grower's motto. This is especially true for perennial producers. Although we can control most grassy weeds with postemergence herbicides, we have few preemergence herbicides that are safe on perennials and no postemergence herbicides to use when broadleaf weeds get out of hand. Furthermore, the preemergence herbicides labeled for use in perennials are either safe on many perennials but don't control many weeds or control lots of weeds but are safe on only a few perennials.

Managing weeds effectively takes a comprehensive program that includes exclusion, sanitation, preemergence herbicides, and hand weeding.

Exclusion and Sanitation

Weed seed and other propagules are introduced into nurseries in the potting substrates, by windblown seed, splashed into pots by rain, deposited by birds, and (perhaps most important) preexisting in the plant materials themselves.

You should inspect new shipments of liners before potting. If you observe weeds that aren't currently present at your nursery, you have two choices: Refuse the shipment or remove the top ½ in. of potting media from the liners and dispose of contaminated media. Closely monitor new plants in the nursery to prevent introduced weeds from going to seed. And cull plants from the nursery that are infested with perennial weeds such as nutsedge.

The worst weed infestations are those that build over time. Weed frequently to keep weeds from going to seed. After hand weeding, remove the weeds from the property. Don't let them go to seed and infest the adjacent pots.

Also, recycled potting media tends to be loaded with weeds. Use recycled media for potting woody ornamentals in which you can use broad-spectrum herbicides.

Preemergence Herbicides

Perennials are sensitive to many of the common nursery herbicides, particularly those that control a broad spectrum of broadleaf weeds.

Scotts Ornamental Herbicide 2, Rout, Regal O-O, and Ronstar all control most weeds in container nurseries but have been shown to injure many perennials. Less efficacious herbicides are more likely to be safe on herbaceous crops but will, of course, not control as broad a spectrum of weeds.

To choose the best herbicide for your nursery, there are two basic strategies to consider: KISS and optimized.

In the KISS (Keep It Simple, Silly) method, you either rely exclusively on hand weeding or you choose a marginally effective preemergence herbicide that's safe on the majority of perennials being grown and supplement that with frequent hand weeding. Research has shown that even a marginally effective herbicide can be cost-effective, reducing the time required for hand weeding.

In an optimized weed control program, you choose the most effective preemergence herbicide labeled for each species. This option requires

Trade name	Active ingredient
Barricade 65 DG or Regalkade 0.5G	**prodiamine**
Fairly broad spectrum of weed control. Safe on many herbaceous ornamentals. Granule is much safer than spray.	
Corral or Pendulum 2G	**pendimethalin**
Fairly broad spectrum of weed control, including annual grasses, spurge, chickweed, and others. Granular formulation is much safer than spray. Safe on many herbaceous ornamentals, but injures some species with foliage that traps granules.	
Devrinol 2G or 5G	**napropamide**
Somewhat narrow spectrum of weeds controlled in containers—primarily annual grasses. Safe on many herbaceous ornamentals but not widely tested on perennials.	
Dimension 1EC or 0.25G	**dithiopyr**
Fairly broad spectrum of weed control when used at the highest labeled rate. Primarily used for crabgrass control in turf but recent label expansion includes many herbaceous ornamentals.	
Snapshot TG	**isoxaben and trifluralin**
Broader weed-control spectrum than the others listed here, but can severely injure several herbaceous perennials (most notably foxglove and most annual bedding plants).	
Surflan, XL	**oryzalin, oryzalin, and benefin**
Broad-spectrum weed control. Safe on several "blue-collar perennials" such as hosta, astilbe, daylily and iris, but the most injurious of the herbicides listed here on many herbaceous perennials. The granular formulation (XL) is much safer than the spray.	
Treflan 5G or Preen	**trifluralin**
Controls annual grasses and a few broadleaf weeds. The weakest weed control of the herbicides listed here, but also the safest herbicide on herbaceous ornamentals. The only species I have injured with Treflan 5G is lantana, which had reduced flower counts but recovered.	

much more planning and on-site experimentation, but it provides the best, most cost-effective weed control. (For information on herbicides for specific crops, consult the sources at the end of this article.)

Due to the tremendous diversity of plants produced in perennial nurseries, the KISS method seems to be the prudent choice for most growers. Larger nurseries, growing greater numbers of each species, may benefit from the optimized approach.

There are some species of herbaceous ornamentals that are even sensitive to our "safest" herbicides. If the herbicide isn't labeled for use on the species you're growing, run small trials before you treat the entire inventory. Also, remember that very young plants are more sensitive to herbicides than older plants, so liner producers will have to rely primarily on sanitation, while finished plant producers can use herbicides more widely. After potting liners, irrigate to settle the soil. The next day, apply the preemergence herbicide to dry foliage and irrigate to incorporate the herbicide into the media and wash it from the foliage.

Remember: No herbicide will control all weeds. Supplement with frequent hand weeding to reduce spread and secondary infestations. Effective herbicide programs will be more effective when combined with diligent sanitation.

Resources: "Weed Control Suggestions for Christmas Trees, Woody Ornamentals, and Flowers" by Skroch, Neal, Derr, and Senesac. AG-427. To order: Send $7.50 (this includes shipping and handling) to Publications, NCSU, Box 7603, Raleigh, NC 27695-7603.

"Weed Management Guide for Herbaceous Ornamentals" by Andrew Senesac. WeedFacts #1. To order: Send $1.25 to WeedFacts, Department of Floriculture and Ornamental Horticulture, 20 Plant Science Bldg., Cornell University, Ithaca, NY 14850.

June 2000

Chapter 6
Marketing

Om Sweet Om

John Friel

So I'm at one of my favorite bars one night recently, the one with live jazz every Sunday. I'm drinking beer, but I like the feeling of hangin' in a classy joint with a wine list the size of a phone book.

I'm telling the bartender about Guinness Stout, that wonderful opaque elixir, the blood of Celtic gods. Sure, he says, we have it. You want a bottle?

No, I tell him, You don't understand: The bottles are okay, but you've gotta have it on tap to really appreciate it. If you can't get it on tap, try the cans. There's this gadget inside, a fizzy little widget that injects nitrogen when you open the can so the stuff has that nice, creamy head just like the draft. That's what you should be serving.

He frowns and shakes his head: I can't have cans in here.

I keep trying to sell him on the idea (old habits die hard.) Look, I ask him, Why wouldn't you want to carry a better product? Heck, I'll buy it. I'm a guaranteed sale every time I walk in here. Even if you stock it just for me, you can't lose.

He's not listening any more. When I stop to catch my breath, he just shakes his head and repeats: I can't have cans in here.

Now it's me who's not listening. I plow on, extolling the virtues of my ancestral brew, appealing alternately to his better nature and his mercenary side. But when I pause to sip the pale ale he's tapped me, he shakes his head again and chants his mantra: I can't have cans in here.

Finally, I get it. His tone is that of a man whose mind is so thoroughly made up, Moses couldn't move him. If the Eleventh Commandment were Thou Shalt Carry Guinness in Cans, he'd be an agnostic. He's encased in his crystal, bulwarked behind his bottles, girded in tradition. And he's making a living. Why mess with it?

So I'm at a trade show a week later, talking with Steve VanderWoude of Spring Meadow Nurseries, a company that continually introduces some of the industry's neatest new shrubs, like *Weigela* 'Wine and Roses' and *Itea* 'Little Henry', to name just a couple.

Steve's laying an anecdote on me about visiting a client whose nursery grows three-gallon containers. The owner loves 'Wine and Roses'. He told Steve that he can sell all the three-gallons he can grow.

That's great, Steve says. But he's trying to convince the owner to try a crop in one-gallon pots, too. Retailers love them, Steve says. They can sell one-gallons all day long to people who want the plant but just won't pay the price for a three.

Yeah, says the owner, But I sell all the three-gallons I can grow.

Steve's not ready to give up. He says, They sell them right alongside their perennials. We did a study where they sold seven times better than perennials—two hundred pots to thirty—when we put them in the perennial section and in the nursery section of the same garden center. You'd still sell all the threes you can grow, and a bunch of ones, too!

Yeah, says the owner, But . . .

You can guess the rest. You've heard the mantra.

No, there's really not a strong link between beer cans and nursery cans, even if they're both black, both nitrogen-injected, and their contents are related in name. The analogy hinges more on our perceptions of ourselves and of our customers.

Yes, it's scary to step out of your comfort zone. Yes, policy, tradition, and consistency are good and necessary things. But successful companies honor their spirit as well as their letter. Look carefully at the shapes of things that don't seem at first glance to fit your tradition. Remember that once upon a time you did for the first time everything you now do every time.

I'm glad Steve's client isn't a bar owner: Much as I love the stuff, even I couldn't drink, or afford, a three-gallon Guinness. But a pint at a time, I'm making Ireland rich. So maybe you're used to getting your money as checks in the mail, or cash over the counter, or by swiping plastic. But if a $50 bill falls from the sky and lands at your feet, do you walk away from it because that's not how you get your money?

Maybe it's time to update your mantra.

December 2001

Perennial Retailers Are "Selling a Promise"

Marketing took front stage at the annual Perennial Plant Association (PPA) Symposium held in Boston, Massachusetts, July 6 to 11.

Speakers drove home the concept that when you sell plants, particularly perennials, you're selling a promise, a hope of what that plant is going to be when it's fully grown. Your job as a retailer is to help your customers visualize that end result.

Speakers also recommended using large picture tags, especially the new locking tags. These new tags stay in place throughout the marketing chain and don't end up scattered on the ground at the garden center after a busy day.

Ian Baldwin, marketing consultant, recommends that retailers create display gardens within their garden centers. "Set up a great-looking sample that has been forced into color so people can see what they'll get from that little, green, scraggly thing potted up on the bench," he told attendees.

Ian also suggested using endcaps as mini-display areas growing larger-sized products providing better training on product knowledge for employees, using plant cards to inform customers, and making a concerted effort to seek out new plants.

Consumers with the largest amount of disposable incomes drive perennial plant buying trends. "Typically, the largest purchasers of gardening materials are those in the forty- to sixty-year-old group," Steve Frowine, president, The Great Plant Company, New Hartford, Connecticut, said in a talk at the symposium.

That age group now is the Baby Boomers, and they'll continue to have the most influence over sales in the general marketplace, Steve said. "We're discovering that they are discriminating, well-educated people with more disposable income. They're often stressed, in a hurry, and have less free time. This means retailers need to provide the information a customer requires to come to a clear decision quickly." And, as Ian Baldwin noted, personal satisfaction has become a major factor for today's consumers. In this day and age, you aren't going to succeed unless your product is "quick, function, or fun."

October 1998

Who Shops for Perennials and What Do They Look For?

Gary Doerr

Peppergrove Nursery, Lapeer, Michigan, surveyed gardeners and non-gardeners to find out about their preferences and expectations when shopping for perennials. Here are highlights from the survey.

Gardeners

- Gardeners are passionate about their hobby and want to be challenged with new, unique, or difficult perennials. Growing perennials is seen as a sign of maturity and "rootedness."
- They crave cultural detail when shopping for perennials.
- Flowers on plants at time of purchase may discourage some gardeners. They get a thrill out of growing and watching the plant mature over time.
- They are disappointed when perennial selection dwindles at the garden center as summer progresses. They want the opportunity to buy fresh, in-prime perennial stock April through October.
- They are aware of branded products and assign value to them.

Non-Gardeners

- Non-gardeners don't fear failure with perennials; they see failure as socially acceptable. At best they will provide minimal care, mostly at planting time.
- Dormant or past-prime perennials are of no interest. Non-gardeners demand action (flowers, foliage) when shopping and selecting.
- Don't bother non-gardeners with cultural detail. "Just the facts, ma'am"—and make it quick. Their mother or friend is viewed as the expert, not the horticulturist.

Gardeners *and* Non-Gardeners

- Both judge quality by cleanliness of the display, selection offered, attitude of the staff, and, yes, the quality of the plant.
- They are wary of a retailer offering a small plant in a big pot.

April 1996

The Right Note

John Friel

Trends in this strange business we're in—the process of manipulating and exploiting the sex lives of members of the vegetable kingdom for our personal gain—tend to mirror trends elsewhere in our culture. Take popular music. Please.

Every emerging musical subgenre—rockabilly, punk, grunge, rap—is first championed by a few groups and hardcore fans and ignored or denounced by the mainstream. But if it sticks around, it gradually affects all music, infusing familiar forms with its signature elements.

The mainstream motto isn't, "If you can't beat 'em, join 'em." It's more like, "If you can't ignore 'em, absorb 'em." Horticulture is no exception. Many growers once considered *perennials* a synonym for *weeds*. Now many of those same growers have trimmed their bedding flats, pruned their rhododendron numbers, and pinched their break-even poinsettia production to accommodate those weeds because perennials are the tune the market is humming.

Result? Woody nurseries and bedding giants plunged into the hardy herbaceous wilderness. Specialty annual programs like The Flower Fields and Proven Winners welcomed perennials and even ornamental grasses into their repertoire. At first glance this may seem like Pat Boone's punk phase, or Streisand releasing a rap CD, except for one little detail: It's working.

A few years ago I was telling people that perennials were at a cross-roads, poised either to plow ahead on the ever-upward path we've forged for two decades, or to hang a hard right onto the boulevard that bedding plants have paved. I was wrong. It wasn't a crossroads—it was an on-ramp, and we're gathering speed.

Forced to place a wager right now, I'd bet that come this date in 2012 there won't be a perennial market and an annual market as we know them today, but a garden plants market.

That makes me nervous. I'm a perennials guy. They're what I know and like, what I've planted and sold. True, we had fuchsias, impatiens, and begonias while I was in sales, but nothing captured my imagination like perennials.

Perennials have stories and traditions, history and mystery. Even their names are fun to say. Just try and say *Matteuccia struthiopteris* without smiling. You can? Oh. OK, say it five times, fast. Better yet, sing it. Thought so. You just don't get a kick like that saying "pansy."

The perennial "fad" has proved to be no such thing. Perennials refused to go away, so the absorption process kicked in. Bedding-plant thinking made inroads among the ranks of perennial growers, and plug factories started learning perennials as a second language.

If, as we go forward, we fuse the best traits of each discipline, we'll all emerge as a hybrid marvel: Think Claude Bolling's "Suite for Flute and Jazz Piano." If we focus on the wrong things, we'll seriously damage consumer confidence in a proven, viable entity: Think Sinatra with a nose ring.

The stakes are high. The best-case scenario will result in really good, garden-worthy, truly hardy perennials; really good, garden-worthy, spec-tacularly colorful annuals; better perennial seed germination rates; and more and more exciting options for gardeners and landscapers.

The wrong-song, wrong-exit scenario will bring us cheap plugs, cheap pots, kamikaze pricing, confused consumers, and volume, volume, volume—and the mindset that says, "Perennials? Just another form of color. No one really cares if it's hardy."

Now, *that's* a wrong note, even if you heard it at the Short Course. Gardeners do too care—a lot. They've told us repeatedly that the selling points of perennials include, for lack of a better term, their "perennialness." Annuals and perennials make wonderful music together in gardens, planters and promotions, but if we want consumers to come back year after year, they have to know which plants will do the same and which won't.

As perennials become more mainstream, those customers who know the least need us the most. The fabled "yardener" allegedly wandering the big-box aisles will open her pocketbook and keep it open, season after season, only if we educate her and help her succeed. That goes beyond packaging: It means being honest about what to expect from our products. She already knows what to expect of perennials. Let's not disappoint her.

Perennial growers, the on-ramp is ending. The tank is full. The Mormon Tabernacle Choir is singing "Highway to Hell." Change the station, check your mirrors and seatbelt, and make it a smooth merge—not a total absorption.

Remember, the sign says "yield," not "surrender."

January 2002

Shorter Is Better

Stephanie Cohen

Being vertically challenged (that's politically correct for just plain short), I tend to be more at eye level with many of the plants I like and admire. The important thing is that short plants generally are front-of-the-border plants and very prominent in the landscape. This requires their foliage to look good from spring to fall, as bad-looking foliage can ruin a garden's appearance. Gardeners are also looking for low maintenance, good seasonality, and few pest or disease problems.

Now that we've set the parameters for good, short, front-of-the-border plants, here are eight interesting border perennials to add to your production list or retail offerings:

Centaurea montana 'Gold Bullion' is a bachelor's button (Zones 4–7) with unbelievable gold to chartreuse leaves that are absolutely startling in color. The larger-than-species flower is a wonderful deep blue, which is an exciting contrast to the foliage. You can plant 'Gold Bullion' in partial sun to full sun. The color, echoing possibilities with yellow-edged hostas such as 'Wolverine', will certainly brighten any shady area. Its June-through-July flowering can make it an exciting combination with *Veronica spicata* 'Icicle', which has large spikes of white flowers and a long bloom season. One of the most popular flower colors in any garden is blue, and this 15-in. plant supplies vibrant color even when not in flower.

Another outstanding newcomer, recently unveiled, elicited oohs and ahs from the perennial gardening market. *Coreopsis rosea*

Centaurea montana 'Gold Bullion'

Coreopsis rosea 'Sweet Dreams'

'Sweet Dreams', a variegated tickseed, is a really hardy perennial (Zones 4–8). All gardeners love daisies, but this little beauty is only 18 in. tall. Picture petals that are white and a dark raspberry that absolutely surrounds the base of the petals. Give this plant full sun and average soil and it will take off—easy as that. Even better, it has finely textured, dark green foliage that serves as an excellent foil to its coloration. As the summer progresses, the raspberry encroaches on the white to show off a kaleidoscope of color. It's a perfect partner to *Leucanthemum* x *superbum*

'Snowcap', a beautiful 18-in. white Shasta daisy, or *Scabiosa columbaria* 'Butterfly Blue', a constant bloomer from June to September, which was also the Perennial Plant of the Year for 2000. The cultivar name for this *Coreopsis* is 'Sweet Dreams', but it will definitely wake up your customers' borders with its great flower power.

Leucanthemum x superbum 'Snowcap'

Scabiosa columbaria
'Butterfly Blue'

Helianthus salicifolius 'Low Down'

Helianthus salicifolius 'Low Down' (Zones 6–9), also known as the willow leaf sunflower, is a full sun plant coming to us from New Zealand. This 12-in. plant, although short in stature, will shake up the fall landscape. I can't describe the foliage because the large daisy flowers completely cover the plant. It's a perfect foil for *Aster amellus* 'Violet Queen' or *Pennisetum alopecuroides* 'Little Bunny' or 'Hameln' (which are both 1 to 2 ft. tall). The fall landscape will never be boring with these outstanding combinations.

Aster amellus 'Violet Queen'

One of the most heat and drought tolerant of all the geraniums is *Geranium himalayense* x *G. wallichianum* 'Rozanne' (Zones 5–8). Mine began flowering in June and was still flowering sporadically in early November. The violet blue flowers have a white eye and wonderfully dissected foliage. In fall it turns autumnal colors of reddish bronze. This is a perfect plant for

Geranium himalayense x *G. wallichianum* 'Rozanne'

front of the border. It looks handsome with *Calamintha grandiflora* 'Variegata'—18 in. tall with pale pink flowers and variegated white and green foliage. You can't beat geraniums for that English cottage garden look.

Last but not least is *Campanula poscharskyana* 'Blue Waterfall', the Serbian bellflower. This is one of my favorite perennials. At just 8 in. tall, this can be used as a wonderful, low-growing groundcover or front-of-the-border winner. The deep blue, bell-shaped flowers with dainty white centers absolutely cover the plant and hide the dark green foliage. The name 'Blue Waterfall' aptly describes how the flowers cascade so freely. This June bloomer flowers profusely for several weeks and

Campanula poscharskyana 'Blue Waterfall'

can flower sporadically into the fall. This plant is classically perfect for edging or for clambering over a rock wall.

All of these perennials will, I'm sure, be received by gardeners and landscapers with enthusiasm and delight, helping them create colorful, carefree, and imaginative borders. Best of all, being compact in size and habit makes them doubly wonderful.

June 2001

Peerless Promotion, Waterloo Gardens Style

Stephanie Cohen

To promote and carve out a special niche for yourself, you must market and advertise. Carl Sturgis, controller of Waterloo Gardens, a retail garden center with locations in Exton and Devon, Pennsylvania, says that 3% of total sales should comprise your advertising budget. My son, who has an MBA degree, has previously taught marketing at Drexel University and is currently product manager for a Fortune 500 software company, says that an advertising budget of up to 10% of gross sales isn't unusual, depending upon your location and your competition.

It takes continuous creative promotion to draw business through your doors.

At Waterloo Gardens, our advertising budget includes:

- Newspaper ads (including tabloids)—45%
- Television—23%
- Radio—15%
- Signage, etc.—10%
- Newsletter—6%
- Web site—1%

Here are some of Waterloo's annual promotions and events and how we market and advertise them.

Newsletters

Our spring newsletter is the big edition of the year, in which we promote new perennials and other green products. Often, this newsletter assists our customers in forming their wish list and also gives them that extra push to get started. In your newsletter, promote your employees. Give them a sense of pride and accomplishment. Many of them have degrees and years of experience. Inform customers about how well trained your staff is.

Another purpose of our newsletter is to offer seminars, workshops, and all types of educational programs to our customers. Keep your customers up-to-date and informed. If you create successful gardeners, then you create good customers.

Signage, regardless of purpose, should be eye-catching and of high quality.

If you have a wholesale business, don't be afraid to do something special for your customers. We offer a two-day educational seminar program to our wholesale customers that's become so successful it's been made available to the Pennsylvania Landscape and Nursery Association for recognized credits for their certification program.

Charitable Festivals

Every spring we host a large garden expo, which opens with an after-hours pre-party grand opening, including food and music. We invite different charitable groups to develop the invitation list, do the mailing, and get a percentage of garden expo sales. Make sure it's a large group that's willing to spend the time to organize the project. They leave happy, and you have made use of a time in your store when it would have normally been closed. Advertise in the newspapers and on radio. Saturate the local stations. Our event is free, and we offer great prizes to draw in the public.

When your store donates to charitable events like Boy Scouts, Girl Scouts, and church groups, have your camera handy. We put some of these events in our newsletter and send pictures to the local press.

Mass Media

We send timely gardening articles to our local press, and they'll print some of them. If you hire a local high school or college graduate, send an announcement to the local newspaper for its local business section for more publicity.

Get Creative—Or Even Wacky

Giveaways, catalogs, coupons, and other events can only add to the excitement and fun of shopping in your store. If you see a newsletter from another area or state with a good idea, "borrow" it and make it better.

In the fall, many of you have Halloween festivals. Consider a German oompah band, a hayride with Johnny Appleseed, a scarecrow-making contest, sing-alongs and storytelling. All these appeal to customers of all ages.

We all love freebies. Customers who wear our perennial-lover T-shirt in July receive a special discount. Meanwhile, they're wearing our name and logo. Or put your logo on baseball caps and give them away. Customers who spend $75 in our gift shop get a special Waterloo Gardens carry bag.

Celebrate anniversaries with your customers. Make them feel like they're a part of your business. Hold contests and sweepstakes to lure them to come and celebrate with you. Send special

T-shirts tied to special sales events can give your store double the promotion.

perennial postcards emphasizing either plants available or garden scenes to demonstrate combinations. Give them plant-buying ideas.

Offer a contest to create a small perennial garden for some lucky homeowner. Blooms of Bressingham is sponsoring just such a promotion. Just remember to take before and after shots for future promotions, and invite your local newspapers and TV channels to the finish of the garden.

Put flyers on parked cars or hand them out at local sports events.

Promote constant sales and markdowns.

Have pickets march outside your store protesting cheap prices.

Avail yourself of all the wonderful Perennial Plant Association handouts. Make up special packets and send them with a coupon to loyal customers.

Advertise children's events. The "Bat Man," the "Bird Man" and the "Butterfly Lady" (local bat, bird and butterfly experts) came to talk to our customers' children. We also promote a special Kids Klub. Children that are kept busy give their parents time to shop. They also develop an interest in gardening, which makes them your future customers.

Offer member discounts to local garden clubs and plant societies. Sponsor a special horticultural award presented to a community member who has done something special for the gardening community.

Host a book signing, along with a discount on the book. If the book happens to be a cookbook on vegetables, herbs, or edible flowers, offer a demonstration with free food.

Publish a colorful catalog packed with ideas and discount coupons and, for additional revenue, charge a nominal fee for it. Promote the catalog on your Web site for added sales.

Create an event to boost sales during slow times. For instance, every year Waterloo has a Perennial Week. This event was designed by David Culp, currently of Sunny Border Nurseries. When he was perennial buyer at Waterloo, he noted our sales dipped between the second and third weeks of June. Now we offer a whole week of seminars and workshops to bring people into the store. In 1999, we featured a tea party to promote our Blooms of Bressingham line of plants. Every year our most popular workshop is run by our propagator, Helen Dennison, who creates a hands-on experience for our customers. She's billed as the "human Ginzu"—she slices and dices. And attendees leave with free plants.

Keeping your customers well informed isn't easy to do. Along with providing a convenient and efficient shopping experience, you need to continually provide information through handouts, newsletters, radio, TV, magazines, and POP to ensure success for your garden center. Make your advertising and marketing plans a reality and a genuine business success by learning to use all avenues available to you. Let them know you're there!

February 2000

Muddy Waters

John Friel

Lawyers know a lot of cute phrases. My favorite goes something like this: "Your Honor, we believe the witness is being less than candid when he says he can't recall why he was in the garden with a shovel at midnight."

Translation: "Liar!"

Lynn Cohen sells perennials wholesale for Sunny Border Nursery in Connecticut, but she has a long background in retail nursery sales. Lynn told me of a visit to a chain store's garden section, where she found big pots of *Mandevilla* 'Alice DuPont'—a splendid vine with large, fragrant, pink flowers and glossy leaves. She watched customers haul them to the cash register. "It must be hardy," one told her companion: "It was with the junipers."

Alas, the many assets of 'Alice DuPont' do not include winter hardiness. She's a tropical vine, a hybrid developed at Longwood Gardens from parent plants native to South America. She loves winter like a squid loves Death Valley. In much of the U.S., poor Alice wouldn't make it to Thanksgiving, never mind Easter.

If this were an isolated incident, it would be just an amusing anecdote in a long list of Stupid Retail Tricks, but many chain employees barely know enough to keep our products alive for a week, let alone give accurate advice about their garden application. The store didn't mean to fool anyone, but nobody knew where the plant belonged. Ignorance does not equal fraud, but the results are the same: dead plants and disappointed consumers.

Ergo, it behooves us all to communicate the pertinent facts about our products. But instead, we're muddying the waters. We're mixing annuals and perennials in borders and containers, we're selling "accent plants" and "tender perennials." We're finding neat new ways to market perennials like asters and campanula as potted flowering houseplants. We're blurring the lines between hardy plants, non-hardy plants, and semi-hardy plants.

This worries me, but not too much. As long as we make each plant's characteristics, including hardiness, absolutely clear to the consumer, I'm fine with mixing and matching. The alternative is either an all-perennials garden or an all-annuals garden, each of which has its weaknesses. The purely-perennials patch lacks the flagrant floriferousness that annuals flaunt all summer; its beauty is of a subtler sort. The annuals-only garden is pure eye candy, but it's a paint-by-numbers deal that looks in September just like it looked in June, only bigger. A perennial border is evolution on fast-forward, a watercolor in the rain, changing weekly as various species segue in and out of bloom—and yearly as its constituents dominate or yield, flourish or succumb, according to their natures.

Perennial gardening is an acquired taste. It's what you grow into after you cut your teeth on annuals, after you realize there's more to life than watering the impatiens again . . . and again and again. But along the way, you'll fall in love with some annuals, too—maybe *Cleome,* maybe a certain *Pelargonium.* And purists be damned—I say throw 'em in there. They'll get along fine.

Today's diversification makes this an enviable time for those of us who love plants for a living and for our chlorophyll-addicted customers. We offer a dazzling rainbow of hue and form. But we also court confusion and disillusionment. There's a lot happening in our industry thanks to new varieties, and a lot of new gardeners discovering the joys of getting their hands dirty. But instead of helping them succeed, we're throwing them a tough learning curve.

A speaker at last year's OFA Short Course showed slides of gorgeous mixed containers—some perennials, some annuals, some herbs—and asked, "Who cares if they're perennials?" Well, we should care because consumers do. I'll bet the ladies who shelled out $30 a copy for 'Alice DuPont' will care a lot when spring returns and Alice doesn't.

A little education and a little plastic—accurate signage and a clear, descriptive pot label—can prevent a lot of misunderstandings. Go ahead and mix up your gardens . . . but not your gardeners.

So you see, Your Honor, we contend that retailers, often unwittingly, are being less than candid with their customers. And we wholesalers who supply them aren't always as forthcoming as we should be, either. When we tell ourselves it's all just "color," we're listening to our bottom line, not to our conscience or to our customers.

Oh, who was it that was selling *Mandevilla,* deliberately or otherwise, as a perennial?

"Gee, I'm sorry, Your Honor, but I just can't remember the store's name. I'm being perfectly, um, candid."

February 2002

How to Effectively Market Perennials

Ellen Talmage and Harlan Hamernik

Obviously, growers market their crops through catalogs, brokers, trade shows, lists, the Web, and, of course, in trade magazines with classified and beautiful display ads. Most in the plant industry take those methods for granted; however, following are half a dozen very effective marketing strategies that many growers overlook.

Trial and Display Gardens at Wholesalers

Many successful growers design, plant, and maintain their own trial and display gardens using a wide range of plant materials. If your crops are perennials, the garden should include bulbs, annuals, vines, shrubs, and trees to showcase your perennial products and offer textures, colors, fragrances, and ideas for combinations throughout the seasons. A design that changes as the months go by helps to attract repeat visitors.

Bluebird Nursery celebrated its 40th anniversary with this flower cake.

At Bluebird Nursery, customers are encouraged to visit the trial and display gardens anytime, but receive a special invitation to attend Field Day, when gardens are at a peak. Special plants are flagged so no one misses them as visitors try to note and photograph their choices from some 3,000 varieties. At Talmage Farm, a display of flowers in vases is maintained in the store with a sign that reads "Plants to See in the Garden."

By having your staff involved in planting, labeling and maintaining the gardens, they develop a sense of pride and, of course, become quite knowledgeable as well as confident.

Display Gardens at Retail

Encourage your retailer customers to also plant display gardens and provide them with plant materials to begin with, as well as design ideas. Show them places and spaces that can be used to display plants, including vines and groundcovers in the ground as well as in containers. Make sure they have colorful flowers and foliage for all seasons.

Remember, their staff needs to learn, too. If we're to enjoy good customers, we must help make them more successful and profitable.

School Landscaping

Help schools and colleges add labeled plants to their campuses, not only for the aesthetic value, but for teaching science, art, agribusiness, etc. Donate or provide plants at a reduced price, especially those plants you grow, and give any needed cultural and design assistance. Make sure children are bit by the gardening bug early, and they'll develop a deep appreciation of plant material. Older students need exposure to a wide variety on an everyday basis to become

potential buyers of our products. Most schools have a teacher or two with some plant knowledge who will be thrilled with such a project.

Opportunity Knocks

Grab every opportunity to talk to the public about your products and how to use them. Provide slides and information to your retail customers to do the same. Homeowners, gardeners, and even novices are starving for plant knowledge and love to hear from the experts.

Clearly, you can't practically prepare a program and talk to every group that calls, but we seldom pass up any interested group of twenty-five to thirty or more potential attendees, even in the busiest of times.

Seminars

Hold educational seminars for your wholesale customers and their plant department staff during winter and very early spring. Provide good, knowledgeable speakers to teach about new and better plants, their uses and best companions, preferred sites, and, of course, how to display and care for them in the garden center or nursery. Customize these classes to meet the needs of individual businesses and their levels of expertise. Remind them tactfully that if they're professionals they must be constantly learning about other ways to use old and new plants.

These seminars are also good times to distribute and make customers aware of the posters and brochures provided by the Perennial Plant Association to help sell. Examples include the "Perennial of the Year" posters and how-to pamphlets such as "Long-Blooming Perennials," "How to Select, Plant and Care for Herbaceous Perennials," and "Perennials for the Shade Garden."

Trade Organizations

Get involved with local, state, national, and international trade organizations. Benefits extend far beyond knowledge gained from leaders in the industry at seminars and tours. Membership lists can be an excellent basis for good customer lists. Conferences are an ideal place to keep in touch with your customers' key people and find new customers. Consider your dues an investment that can provide huge dividends from networking opportunities, marketing publications, etc. Successful marketing programs can make an excellent grower into an outstanding business; don't miss the opportunities that are out there!

The Perennial Plant Association (PPA) is one group that is dedicated to improving the perennial plant industry by providing education to enhance the production, promotion, and utilization of perennial plants. More information on membership and promotional material can be obtained from PPA by writing to them at 3383 Schirtzinger Road, Hilliard, OH 43026, or e-mailing ppa@perennialplant.org.

June 1999

When Is a Perennial New and Not Just a New Name?

Many longtime perennial growers know that in the world of new varieties, very few new perennials developed from breeding programs are introduced each year. However, it seems that some years, growers can find hundreds of "new" perennials offered by suppliers.

Why is that? Sometimes companies rename an existing variety on the market so it'll look different, and sometimes a company will introduce a new species to cultivation, putting a marketing name on the plant and promoting it as a new product from breeding, says Georg Uebelhart, general manager for perennial specialist Jelitto Stau-densamen, Schwarmstedt, Germany. "Renaming varieties isn't ethical," Georg says. "People ask for novelties; [supply] companies need novelties. To breed, you have to work for five to ten years to have a truly new variety."

Jelitto's own breeding program has given the perennial industry many new products. Probably their most famous is *Echinacea purpurea* 'Magnus', the Perennial Plant Association's Perennial of the Year for 1998. An improved 'Magnus', with even darker crimson flowers, has also been bred. Other perennials from Jelitto's own breeding program include *Achillea sibirica* 'Love Parade', *Echinops* 'Arctic Glow', *Polemonium boreale* 'Heavenly Habit', *Sedum spurium* 'Summer Glory', and *Verbascum phoeniceum* 'Violetta'.

"The perennial market is small, and there are more new varieties promoted than have actually recently been 'bred'; a lot of renames and a lot of adding a marketing name to a species to make it sell better," Georg says. *Rudbeckia* 'Goldsturm', a mainstay for growers in many temperate climates, is a good example. The species was discovered before World War II, but what excitement is there in a variety called *Rudbeckia fulgida* variety *sullivantii*? 'Goldsturm' was added as a selling name.

Jelitto's breeding program is looking at applying a series approach to mainstays: producing a range of colors in a series, as is done with bedding plants.

What's hot right now? Perennials sold for pot plant sales, in color. Worldwide, *Lavendula* is one of their largest selling genera. Perennial sales are stable in Europe, but growing rapidly in Japan and the U.S.

Jelitto works with more than three hundred contract growers in Chile, Europe, Japan, New Zealand, and the U.S. to produce seed. Their research lab adds value to seed through the Gold Nugget program, where seeds are pretreated, thus increasing germination counts and speed of germination for plug and young plant suppliers and growers. About 100 of Jelitto's 2,500 items are currently offered as Gold Nugget. You can contact Jelitto at Fax: (502) 895-3934 or Online: www.jelitto.com.

March 2000

Bumper Crop

John Friel

The persons who asked the following questions will not be identified, except one—me. Some are still customers; some have mercifully disappeared into the Witless Protection System.

I'll go first.

"Who's gonna buy one of these? Nobody!"—Yours truly, circa 1958. Subject: The Volkswagen Beetle.

Dad was Ford man. His first car was a Model T; his last, a 1963 Country Squire, a behemoth with fake wood sides and a three-acre hood covering enough engine to power a small factory. That V-8 burned oil like a two-stroke and sucked hi-test like a fraternity processing beer.

One day, Dad swapped cars with a friend who was moving furniture. The friend got Dad's '57 Ford wagon, the Squire's predecessor, and Dad got the friend's VW, the first Bug in town.

Dad piled us in and off we went in that tin box, listening to the tiny engine roaring incongruously behind us. It had a split rear window, no gas gauge, no radio. For turn signals, a little stick would flip out of the side and point the way you intended to turn.

And I laughed my six-year-old butt off. I just knew the VW we were riding in would be the only one ever sold.

OK, let's embarrass someone else for a while. We'll come back to me.

"Perennials . . . are those the ones that come up every year, or is that annuals?"—Too many to list. Haven't heard this one in years, but it was a common phone query when we started growing these odd things. If you're still not sure, try Henry Beard's definition: "Perennial: Any plant which, had it lived, would have bloomed year after year."

"When do you stop shipping?"—Again, too many to list. The question speaks volumes about how perennials were bought, sold, produced, and shipped back in the day: Big woody cuttings, sand beds, sawdust, wooden crates. Ship till they're gone, then shut down, take a break, start over.

The answer then was, "When we run out." The answer now is, "We don't." Perennials ship every week of the year now. This question dates from a time when this business had lulls, when perennials were just finding their identity as something more than the bastard child of the nursery and greenhouse industries. We've still got a foot in each world, but we wear our hybrid colors proudly now.

"Perennials don't die. Why would anyone come back for more next year?" The correct, if impolite, answer here is, "Do you always answer your own question before you ask it?" People come back for more because they don't die.

"Who wants a coral bells that ain't got no coral bells?"—A famous Maryland nurseryman, spurning my efforts to sell him *Heuchera* 'Palace Purple' in the mid '80s. Answer: Everybody. This PPA Plant of the Year spawned a new and still-flourishing career for its genus, as a foliage accent whose flowers are a bonus or an afterthought.

"Perennials don't need maintenance, right? You just plant 'em, and they take care of themselves year after year." Answer: Right, and ditto for children and pets. This idea was promulgated by landscapers who went on to lucrative careers in real estate and used car sales. Wanna buy a bridge? How about an Edsel?

"Why do you keep dropping plants and adding new ones? I just got my customers used to that other one!"—Asked circa 1982 by a New Guinea impatiens buyer, bemoaning our switch from 'Mohawk' to 'Red Planet', neither of which would survive today's bedding/basket market. Too leggy, too thirsty, too spindly; flowers too few and too small.

Henry Ford nearly ruined the huge company he'd built from scratch by clinging to the Model T. Other automakers leapfrogged past him with better, safer, faster cars, while Henry—grudgingly—offered the T in different colors.

But I digress . . . or do I? Why do we drop, add, and improve? To survive. Which brings us back to the car swap. OK, kids, get out.

Twenty years later, I was the proud owner of a VW bus not much newer than that original tiny tin box. Collectively, my siblings and offspring and I have owned about a dozen VW products.

Ponder that, dear reader, and consider the source whenever this column dares augur our industry's future. Ponder that, symposium organizers, next time you seek a lecture on trends.

Happy motoring.

March 2002

More Turns This Summer

Stephen Still

Garden center sales of perennials are very much like the high school prom. You plan all winter and spring and then one day in May it's all over. A goal of the retailer is to extend past that glorious day in May and sell perennials through the summer. This is what has led to the Perennial Plant Association creating a " June is Perennial Gardening Month" (JPGM) promotion. It's even been registered with Chase's Calendar of Events (www.chases.com).

JPGM is a product of the Marketing and Promotion Committee of the PPA. The reason for launching this promotion was to extend the "active" selling season of perennials past the normal April and May peak season. This will require an educational and promotional effort directed toward growers, retailers, and, of course, consumers. PPA feels that as the consumer market becomes aware of the pleasures of stretching out the gardening season through the summer and fall months, the increased demand for perennials will in effect give growers another perennial turn or two. And, of course, garden centers will be engaging more customer traffic and selling more perennials for a longer period of time.

Make It POP

During the first year of the program, the majority of the effort has been directed toward assisting the retailer. We've developed POP materials to assist in promotion. The lead item is a 2-by-3-ft. June Is Perennial Gardening Month poster ($2.75 for PPA members for one to twenty-four posters; $4.75 for nonmembers,). The colorful poster highlights individual perennials as well as several perennial combinations. 'Becky' Shasta daisy, 'Happy Returns' daylily and 'Six Hills Giant' catmint are examples of selected perennials on the poster. The 2001 Perennial Plant of the Year, 'Karl Foerster' feather reed grass, is another poster feature. Retailers can use the poster to highlight displays of June-flowering plants or to complement their Perennial Plant of the Year posters. Growers can buy the inexpensive posters and provide them with shipments going to retailers.

An 8½-by-11-in. glossy, color flyer also will be available for retailers and growers ($0.10 each for members in any quantity; $0.12 for nonmembers). This flyer is similar to the poster, with text on the reverse side. The text material is directed toward the consumer with information on bed preparation, maintenance ideas and suggested perennials and perennial combinations to be used in June and later in the summer. These flyers are perfect for including in direct mailing pieces to your garden center customers.

The Perennial Plant Association hopes its new program will help you boost summer sales. Flyers, postcards, and posters are part of PPA's new POP offerings. Watch for the program to expand for 2002.

A four-color postcard and a June newsletter will also be available ($0.20 each in any quantity; members get 10% discount). The postcard, illustrating a June perennial combination, is suitable for mailing to customers to announce special programs, sales, and other information about your JPGM promotion. All of the POP carries a special JPGM logo that's been developed for this campaign. Retailers can obtain the postcard with custom printing on the back or with no printing.

The JPGM June newsletter will contain two inside pages of text prepared by the PPA, including suggestions of plants for June bloom and maintenance tips for June. The outside two pages of the newsletter will be available for custom printing. Both the postcard and newsletter can be used to announce June is Perennial Gardening Month.

Extending Your Season

How can retailers use this information to their advantage to increase perennial traffic this summer? Here are a few ideas:

Festivals

There are many reasons for a festival or open house in June and during the summer. How about a June is Perennial Gardening Month open house? This could occur on a single weekend, or some retailers are highlighting all four weekends as perfect times to obtain those June-flowering perennials.

Plum Creek Gardens, Oconomowac, Wisconsin, is planning a second annual June promotion after experiencing success in 2000, when they first developed a Perennial Festival for late June. It was promoted by flyers sent to customers and bold advertisements in local papers. Specials were run on hostas and perennials, with a main emphasis on the Perennial Plants of the Year (PPOY). Customers were able to purchase a special package of all eleven Perennial Plants of the Year. Educational workshops highlighted maintenance and division of perennials. Barbara Barnes reports that "it made us realize how many people are just learning about perennials and are so eager to participate." Customer responses included, "I hope you have this program every year!" Barbara adds that they experienced four times more business than anticipated. This June, Plum Creek Gardens' festival theme will be Summer of Color and will highlight perennials that bloom from late spring to fall. The POP materials for June is Perennial Gardening Month will be excellent tie-ins.

PPOY promotions

Many perennials selected as Perennial Plant of the Year selections are June-flowering perennials. *Astilbe* 'Sprite', *Salvia* 'May Night', *Scabiosa columbaria* 'Butterfly Blue', and *Calamagrostis* x *acutiflora* 'Karl Foerster' are all PPOY selections that flower in June. Of course there are others, such as *Rudbeckia* 'Goldsturm' and *Echinacea* 'Magnus' that can be promoted for summer blooms.

Perennial of the week

To gain the maximum exposure for JPGM, you can promote a perennial for each week during June. End caps and displays might include various species and cultivars of a specific June-flowering genus. List the specials on your direct mail postcard.

Perennial walk

For retailers with display gardens or exhibits, schedule a monthly perennial walk to show your customers how the garden changes through the summer. Planting the display garden to include June- and later-flowering perennials will keep customers coming back to the garden center on a regular basis.

Hands-on seminars

Scheduling weekly programs related to perennial gardening is a good way to promote JPGM. Short programs to illustrate pruning, mulching, proper bed preparation, and general plant care are great ways to increase garden center traffic. At this point, the key is to have well-grown perennials available for purchase. Don't close down your perennial selection availability after Memorial Day. It's important that growers have healthy, fresh, mature perennials available to ensure that consumers are getting the best plants possible. You don't want to be promoting JPGM with substandard plants. PPA has distributed press packets to garden writers and media members of the National Gardening Bureau, so watch for stories in magazines and your local newspapers. Contact them directly and tell them about any special promotions you're doing.

Planning for 2002 is already underway. In addition to the poster, flyer, and direct mail post card, a gardening calendar for June will be developed for use by consumers. The calendar will provide a list of perennial gardening activities for June.

To order any of the POP materials, call the Perennial Plant Association at (614) 771-8431, fax them at (614) 876-5238, or check them out online at www.perennialplant.org.

June 2001

Cyberspuds

John Friel

Ever wonder why there are so many Irishpersons in America? Cops named Clancy, politicians named Kennedy, dairypersons named O'Leary, writers named Friel? We have a microorganism to thank: *Phytophthora,* the little bugger that causes fungal root rot in a host of greenhouse crops.

P. infestans caused Ireland's famous potato famines of the 1800s, killing a million Irish poor and triggering the exodus of another 2.5 million to England, Europe, Australia, and North America. In just a couple of decades, Ireland's population was halved. Those dark days are known in Ireland as "The Great Hunger"—*An Gorta Mor* in Gaelic, the native tongue that was nearly wiped out when the famine killed off those who spoke it.

Among the factors that made these particular infestations so horrific was that nearly all of Ireland was planted in one variety of potato, the lumper. Another variety, the cup, was also grown. (My marketing reflexes make me wonder what the focus group was drinking when they picked those names.)

By any name, both varieties succumbed to the root rot, and square miles of potato crops turned to black mush. With them went a race that depended almost entirely upon them for food, tossed into mass graves from Killarney to Dundalk.

Why do I mention this, other than that it's St. Patrick's Day as I type? What triggered it was the antivirus software message that flashed on my screen when I booted up a bit ago. Yes, it's a bit of a stretch from spuds to PCs. (No, this half-baked analogy has nothing to do with chips. Nice try, though.)

That McAfee moment brought back a conversation from last fall, a conversation held while rafting down the Colorado River through Grand Canyon, reading Michael Pollan's *The Botany of Desire* in calm stretches, tucking it away in a waterproof bag as we plunged through rapids. Another hort type and I got into a conversation about the book, and about the dangers of monoculture—how relying on a single susceptible species or variety leaves growers vulnerable, whether their crop is potatoes or poinsettias or phlox. And a third party chimed in, straight out of left field, that IBM's dominance in the computer world amounts to an electronic monoculture, leaving us all vulnerable to various viruses, worms, Trojan horses, and other acts of e-terrorism devised by clever folks with too little conscience and too much time on their hands.

He made a startlingly apt point. Putting all your eggs, or spuds, in a single basket is a dangerous habit. Ask anyone who bet the ranch on Enron stock, or committed three-quarters of his production to a chain that went Chapter 11. Diversity is a good thing—in a portfolio, in computers (hardcore Mac users can get downright smug about how few viruses infest their little world), in your customer base, and certainly in a growing program.

Diversity is the perennial market's main strength. Perennial growers can't survive growing a Top 20 list any more than Ireland made it on lumpers and cups. So we stay hungry. We search obsessively for new genera, new species, new cultivars. Every year we crowd the rail as some promising new item appears on the horizon like Liberty's torch rising from the curved sea.

I recommend Pollan's book, by the way; at his best he's among the finest in his field, nearly as readable as Allen Lacy. And I highly recommend rafting the Colorado, too. But experiencing the two simultaneously is too incongruous; it's distracting to picture fields of tulips while drifting through hundreds of miles of desert, past cliffs decorated with yuccas, scorpions, big-horn sheep, and the traces of ancient civilizations who somehow wrung a living from that stingy environment. One wonders if the Anasazi could somehow have survived *An Gorta Mor.*

So many of my ancestors did not; just enough did. It's edifying, if not particularly ego-bolstering, to ponder that were it not for a microorganism, and a nasty one at that, I wouldn't exist. But there it is. And here we are, the cops and the pols, the dancers and the writers, the coal miners and the singers. The potato crop has long since been rebooted, with chemical shields and resistant strains.

Still, we're all vulnerable to one form of attack or another—viruses, fungi, the bankruptcies of others. So keep your eyes peeled for villains both micro and macro, be they old ones like *Phytophthora infestans* or new ones like hackdaddy@vandals.com. And also for new opportunities, and new baskets.

May 2002

Tour Stops Highlight Perennial Marketing Ideas

Cathy St. Pierre

For sixteen years, the Perennial Plant Association (PPA) Symposium has provided a forum for the exchange of ideas for perennial growers, retailers, and other professionals. This year's symposium was held in Boston, Massachusetts, July 6 to 11, with more than nine hundred registrants attending tours and seminars, the largest attendance to date. Seminar topics ranged from overwintering to creating tropical effects using hardy perennials.

Tours let attendees take a firsthand look into the operations of wholesale growers, garden centers, and some of the most beautiful perennial gardens in New England. Here are the highlights from five innovative retailers we visited:

Blanchette Gardens, Carlisle

Blanchette Gardens, Carlisle, was started in 1981 by Leo and Pam Blanchette. Their sales area, which doubles as a growing area, feels like a combination of a garden center, botanical garden, and research center. Customers are just as likely to come equipped with cameras and notepads as with children and strollers. *The Boston Globe* has noted this nursery as the best for shade-loving perennials.

With 130 varieties of *Astilbe*, Blanchette Gardens caters to collectors and seems like a combination of a garden center, botanical garden, and research center.
Photo by Christina St. Pierre.

The Blanchettes cater to the collector, offering an extensive list of perennials, including many rare and new varieties. "I don't know anybody else who produces the diversity that we do," says Leo. For example, they carry 130 varieties of astilbe, over 40 varieties of ferns, and even a shade-loving peony. "We like to do the odd-ball stuff," says Leo. Some of his plants start from seed gathered on their trips abroad or received from botanists from as far away as Russia.

The sales area has 100,000 containers laid out in neat, numbered blocks that allow plants to be found easily with catalog in hand. Every single variety has its own 4-by-6-in. laminated card detailing identifying characteristics and precise nomenclature. "I do my best to stay current," says Leo. "The scientist in me wants to be accurate, but the nurseryman in me goes crazy." The cards provide a low-cost, mobile way of providing information to the consumer. Leo figures the signs cost him $.08 each. He produces them himself during the winter with the use of his computer and laminating pouches. He estimates it takes about forty hours to complete the cards for an entire season.

This simple and effective system was prompted as much by necessity as by scientific fervor. Leo and Pam run the whole business—Leo propagates 90% of their plants (that's over 40,000 cuttings between April 1 and mid-July), and Pam does all the sales. That means they are available to customers for a limited amount of time and need to use that time to answer questions that can't be answered any other way.

Briggs Nursery, North Attleboro

Briggs Nursery began in 1961 as a family-owned landscape design firm with some nursery stock in a small retail area. In the 1980s, they expanded their retail garden area, which now accounts for more than 85% of their revenues. And within retail, perennials account for the largest sales increases over the past several years. For this reason, they're expanding their perennial selection. As with most garden centers in the Northeast, acquiring additional acreage to accommodate additional crops isn't really an option; instead they've begun the process of optimizing their existing space by moving or taking down sheds, repaving lots, and reorganizing display beds.

In 1997, General Manager Gary Briggs toured many of England's garden centers and was impressed by both the looks of their garden centers and how they retail their merchandise. The English place a heavier emphasis on marketing and merchandising and received more support from the companies that supply them with product. Last year, Briggs became a key stockist for Blooms of

Briggs Nursery demonstrates a strong English influence in its look, layout, and merchandising.
Photo by Christina St. Pierre.

Bressingham and has put into use many of the POP displays, ad slicks, and oversized color tags that are part of Blooms' merchandising program.

English garden centers are often beautiful as well as functional. At Briggs, over 150 elegant wood benches have replaced standard wire mesh tables. The grounds are set up so customers can enjoy and experience what can be done to beautify their properties. A well-established annuals display garden gives bedding plant ideas; the shade garden created last year is expanding to include ferns and native plants; and more areas are being cultivated with stone walls laid out around them. Plans are underway to add sun borders, a grass garden, a rock/alpine garden, and a cottage garden.

Over time, Briggs has steadily met its goal of becoming a "destination" gardening source. "We try to offer everything a novice or experienced gardener would need," says Gary. The main store has 6,500 sq. ft. of retail stock; hardgoods cover everything from statuary to bulk materials; and there's also a florist and nursery. If parents bring the children along, there's a petting zoo and playground to meet their needs, too.

Mahoney's Garden Center, Winchester

Mahoney's-Rocky Ledge at Winchester is the largest of the family's three garden center locations. This second-generation, family-run business ranks in the country's top fifty for volume of sales. Gross sales of perennials alone at the Winchester location total over $700,000 per year.

Retailing methods at each site reflect the market particular to that area. Where Mahoney's-Rocky Ledge is expansive and low-key, Mahoney's-Cambridge is concentrated and high energy. At Rocky Ledge, where the PPA toured, visitors move from the lush and sometimes exotic look of annuals in retail houses, past the earthiness of the nursery material, to the homey atmosphere of the perennials and their growing houses.

Posted within the perennial sales area are product lists referencing each variety by name and matching bench number. A variety of directories and ample signage assist customers in locating and choosing between the 1,500 varieties.

A variety of directories and ample signage assist customers in locating and choosing between the 1,500 perennial varieties stocked by Mahoney's Garden Center.
Photo by Cathy St. Pierre.

According to Mahoney's staff, consumers today expect perennials to perform in many ways that have traditionally been the job of annuals: longer bloom times, greater color, and more novel flower and plant forms. For example, customers are more and more interested in varieties like *Coreopsis* 'Flying Saucer', which will bloom a deep gold color all season, compared with the limited color of *Coreopsis* 'Early Sunrise'.

Other trends include rediscovery of older varieties of common species (such as Shasta daisy 'Becky'), increased interest in shade materials (due in part to the building up of the urban environment), and a move to larger, more mature potted plants that provide instant gratification—a reflection of the fast-paced, time-crunched lifestyle of the suburbanite.

Weston Nurseries, Hopkinton

Founded in 1923, Weston Nurseries covers over nine hundred acres. And while most of their acreage is nursery growing space, sales over the past ten years have shifted from primarily wholesale to a 50/50 whole-sale/retail mix. They believe that the extraordinary building boom that the Boston suburbs have experienced has greatly influenced this change in the marketplace.

Presently, their greatest challenge has come in the form of the mass merchandiser, which has grabbed the low end, low service segment of the market. Weston Nurseries has chosen to distinguish itself through a blend of product, service, and "experience."

First, product lines have moved from commodity items such as white pine to more unusual products, through constantly searching out new varieties and developing hybrids. Because they grow what they sell, they can maintain a high standard of quality control and offer as wide a selection of plant material as the customers demand.

Maintaining a high degree of customer service and support has meant building a highly educated sales staff and a system to keep them as accessible to customers as possible. One idea they've implemented addresses the frustration of finding a salesperson in the

Weston Nurseries has chosen to distinguish itself through a blend of product, service, and "experience." One experience is an extensive and detailed garden railway.
Photo by Christina St. Pierre.

free-for-all atmosphere of spring and busy weekends. One of the staff suggested the idea of a paging system. When a customer comes in, they register at the "podium." All staff report back to the podium when they have finished with a customer and are assigned to the next customer on the list, who is contacted by loudspeaker. This has eliminated much of the stress and uncertainty for the customer and smoothed out busy days.

"The 'experience' is the way to go," says Tom Strangfeld, Weston's director of sales and marketing. Creating an unusual and engaging shopping environment is something the mass marketers have yet to master. Within the retail selling area, there are any number of activities going on. One of the most fascinating for adults and children is an elaborate garden railway, complete with tiny houses, a church, watering hole with fishermen, and even the local diner. Constructed along a grade in the garden center, the train winds through tunnels, climbs multiple levels along miniature hillsides, and traverses ravines over trestle bridges. Holding it all together is a landscape of plant material chosen for their ability to fit the scale of the make-believe town. Small shrubs become trees and tiny annuals become shrubs.

Other areas under development include restoration of a 1790s farmhouse enclosed within a "period" display garden, an Asian-style meditation house, and trails through the nursery production areas.

Windy-Lo Nursery, Natick

Charm. That says it all. When customers pull into the parking area at Windy-Lo, they're transported to another place and time, one where cozy benches are nestled in beds of color, and a country house is framed within a tumble of perennials. The cottage doubles as a country store where children can buy penny candy while parents shop for gardening supplies.

Windy-Lo is located in the Boston suburbs and has twenty-two acres total, fifteen of which are retail. Sally Flagg, a member of the family who started and runs this family-owned business, counts location as a major factor in the nursery's success. With little competition in the immediate area, this is true. What isn't revealed is the wonders they've done with this location. Just ten minutes away, commuters are jammed in rush hour traffic, heading into Boston. In contrast, Windy-Lo is a warm and welcoming haven, right down to Ben, the resident black Labrador retriever, who greets customers as they enter along the brick walkway.

Information is readily at hand throughout the retail area. Signs in the gazebo list plants by their common and botanical names. Others list plants according to function such as sun, shade, and butterfly and hummingbird attracting. Plant locations are clearly mapped and easily found.

Creative plant combinations in window boxes and containers offer a host of ideas to customers. Theme gardens in the retail area are often constructed of potted material that can be picked up and purchased.

Windy-Lo has built strong customer loyalty through excellent customer service and support, offering loading service, personal attention, and a lot of information. Sally sees their business as

Windy-Lo Nursery's niche is being a warm and welcoming haven for harried Boston commuters.
Photo by Christina St. Pierre.

the perfect size for the market: "Small enough to serve the customers personally and large enough to satisfy their appetites."

September 1998

Affairs of the Mart

John Friel

My friends Doug and Lisa used to play a game at parties where they knew hardly anyone. They'd separate, mingling with other guests. Then Doug would reappear. Leering like Groucho, he'd sidle up close and initiate the following dialogue:

DOUG: "Would you sleep with me for a million dollars?"

LISA (blushing): "Well . . . yes, I guess I would."

DOUG: "How about for twenty bucks?"

LISA (furious): "Certainly not! What kind of girl do you think I am?"

DOUG: "We've already established that. Now we're just haggling over the price."

That old joke comes to mind when I ponder the complex interface between perennial growers and big-box stores.

Disclaimer: My employer is a major supplier to major suppliers to the mega-retailers, so if you're looking for big-box bashing, look elsewhere. I mention this because it's the ideal perspective from which to view the monolith: close enough to be conversant with issues, detached enough to be objective about them.

Every grower (and I don't mean only perennial growers, I mean all growers, whether you produce *Baptisia* or begonias) knows deep down that you can't grow it for a buck, sell it for ninety-nine cents, and make it up in volume. You don't need some wise-guy columnist to drill you in basic math.

But by their sheer magnitude, the numbers a big retailer can whisper in a supplier's ear have a hypnotic effect, and growers in our industry can be especially susceptible. Many of us still aren't accustomed to the idea that perennials are no longer a kinky little niche in the edifice of ornamental horticulture. We've arrived, but we don't always act like it or price like it.

One must, of course, try to understand one's customer and one's customers' customers and be sensitive to their associated needs. But sensitivity, like all good things, can be overindulged in. If you grow for a chain, one of your most keenly felt needs is to keep your price low. If your customer grows for a chain . . . well, you get the picture:

"This new buyer is really squeezing me," your customer says. "You gotta help me keep this account. What can you do for me?" And the next thing you know, your margin has become his margin. You've fixated on that big shiny total. You've turned a blind eye to the reality of the merchandising burden suppliers must shoulder to play in the big ballparks—delivery on demand, special tagging, plant maintenance, penalties for slipups, copayments for regional advertising—and said yes too easily. He knows what kind of girl you are, and the rest is just details.

Price point pressure, slavishly obeyed, is the enemy of both profit and quality, and it won't stay put. Like kudzu, it creeps off the retailer/grower negotiating table and snakes its way up the supply channel. And total capitulation threatens the whole food chain. It leadeth us out of the black and into the red-tinged valley of the vanishingly small margin or into a mindset that results in only cheap, easy-to-produce perennials on the shelves. The latter scenario shows better math skills, but less grasp of the strengths of the perennial market.

Those strengths are quality, diversity, and new plants. Producing a good mix of quality perennials, with a healthy dose of exciting new introductions, takes a significant expenditure of both resources and resourcefulness. There are millions to be made in the big-box bed if you mind that margin; but growing easy, familiar perennials and focusing only on the bottom line cheats both the industry and the consumer.

Fortunately, despite a few horror stories, smart buyers aren't out to bankrupt their suppliers. They want the good ones back year after year, the ones who ship quality product on time, reliably—the ones whose *Gaura* scans as readily as a pack of gum; the ones whose stuff demonstrates good "sell through."

If your perennials and your style fit those criteria, you'll be treated well. But buyers will negotiate very hard, and you'd better know the exact location of the line that separates positive from negative. We've seen good growers driven to distraction and the brink of fiscal catastrophe because they promised too much for too little.

Moral: Beware of the familiar stranger. Know your true costs of production and merchandising. Be careful with whom you climb into bed—and at what price.

November 2001

Chapter 7
Grower Profiles

Dynamite in Gallon Pots
Debbie Hamrick

Perennials now account for 26.6% of all U.S. outdoor flowering plant sales, with $642 million wholesale among 7,391 producers. Demand has been soaring for the past decade, and according to our informal poll of two dozen growers, garden center and mass-market retailers, and perennial young plant suppliers and breeders, the boom is far from over. There are plenty of under-exploited opportunities for growers looking for smart ways to position themselves in perennials.

To give you some ideas, we're providing you with major trends for the perennial market on everything from infrastructure issues such as young plant supply to production topics and retail displays. Sprinkled in, you'll find vignettes on some of America's best growers and suppliers, all companies who are succeeding with a focused approach to their specific markets.

Perennials: The Great Industry Equalizer
Perennials are helping to blur the lines between the segments of ornamental horticulture because everyone is growing them: greenhouse growers, perennial specialists, and nurserymen. While perennial specialists have dominated in the past, greenhouse growers are rapidly moving in. The major difference? Crop turns. Greenhouse growers understand the concept of rapidly turning crops because they know that every turn adds incrementally to bottom-line profit.

Perennial specialists have tended to grow more like nurserymen, with a "plant it and keep it in inventory" philosophy. Many average fewer than two turns overall per year. Greenhouse growers, who view perennials as a way to make their assortment a one-stop shopping experience for customers and to extend "shoulder season" sales before and after main bedding plant sales, average much higher turns across their production area. The greenhouse grower segment has also introduced the concept of in-store servicing of displays for perennials, pioneered by companies such as Ivy Acres, Long Island, New York, and Stacy's Greenhouses and Nurseries, York, South Carolina.

We're also starting to see more formalized approaches to the blurring of perennials, annuals, and spring plants. Skagit Gardens, Mt. Vernon, Washington, is banking on what they call a "zone denial" approach to mixing perennials with annuals in their potted spring lines. And thousands of growers working with Proven Winners' Fall Magic program are enjoying a brand-new sales season, using an approach that mixes perennials with pansies and other annuals. And a large number of young plant and plug suppliers now offer perennials such as lavender, hardy verbenas, gauras, and salvias along with their annual liners.

Alliances, such as between Yoder Green Leaf and The Paul Ecke Ranch's Flower Fields and between InnovaPlant (Proven Winners) and Terra Nova, will further speed and formalize the blurring of the lines of separating annuals and perennials. Growers will also have access to increased POP and tagging opportunities through these programs and others, such as Ball Seed's new Lasting Beauty program.

Self-Propagation Still Popular

Since perennials encompass such a broad range of plants, young plant supply can be problematic. For this reason, many growers self-propagate as well as buy in young plants. Part of the reason some growers self-propagate has to do with their mentality: That's the way it's always been done. Also, maintaining stock plants and ensuring that plants are true-to-name has been an issue at times. But three factors will change this paradigm.

First is that major players such as Yoder Green Leaf are initiating rigorous stock maintenance programs that ensure plants are not only true-to-type, but also free of latent virus and disease. Second, as the number of patented, vegetatively propagated plants continues to increase, distribution will be more tightly controlled. Growers won't simply be able to propagate plants at will; royalties will be involved. Finally, liner and plug suppliers continue to further refine their vernalized programs for crops requiring cold treatment. As this option becomes more popular, growers can get plants in and finish them within a few weeks, rather than potting them up, growing them on for five or six months, and then selling them.

Bareroot plants remain the most popular way for most growers to produce leading plants like *Hosta, Hemerocallis, Iris,* and *Paeonia.* The advent of tissue culture labs has exacerbated an oversupply of some bareroot varieties, especially *Hosta,* as anyone looking for large quantities of common hostas discovered last summer: Prices were at or below production costs.

Since bareroot plants take so long to produce (many take one year or more), timing of specific varieties into the marketplace is an imprecise science at best. Perhaps that's why some of the country's leading bareroot suppliers are also turning to plug and liner production, so they can increase the types of plants offered for sale and have more flexibility in the quantities and timing.

Tissue culture allows rapid increase of stock plants. That, in turn, allows breeders and young plant suppliers to ramp up their cutting production quickly, which means that new varieties can get into the marketplace in much larger numbers much faster than ever before. Combine the ability to rapidly introduce new varieties with good marketing and promotion, and it's almost certain the perennial scene will dramatically change in the coming years.

Even with all this excitement, there are still no formalized perennial trialing programs. Some breeders work with a few scattered universities and botanical gardens, but there are no formalized outdoor trialing programs across a wide range of climates. Consequently, every young plant supplier, grower, retailer, and consumer who purchases a new variety or previously unknown plant becomes a guinea pig. Ask a smattering of retailers what really bugs them about perennials, and this is an area where you'll get an earful. Growers who want to earn the undying love and respect from their customers will plant trial gardens to get a true look at how specific plants perform in the regions they sell to.

Controversial Timing

Work being done at Michigan State University is helping some growers do a better job getting flowering perennials into the marketplace when large numbers of consumers are predisposed to buying them—in the spring. By breaking the large group of perennials into "response" groups, such as plants with obligate long-day or short-day requirements or vernalization requirements, growers can time plants to flower together. Getting *Sedum* 'Autumn Joy', *Rudbeckia* 'Goldsturm', or *Echinacea* 'Magnus' onto the retail shelf in flower in April isn't just possible, it's being done. And MSU's field trials have demonstrated that "forced" plants can and do perform when planted outdoors. Some even reflower during their "normal" season when planted the same year they're purchased.

To many long-time perennial production community members, putting plants into the market out-of-season is highly misleading to consumers, who they say will expect plants to flower at the same time next year. To others, putting plants in flower on the retail shelf allows consumers the opportunity to "see" what they're buying. The controversy is far from over.

Any retailer will tell you one thing: "If it's in color, it walks." Yet very few growers seem to have digested that fact. Retailers want plants staged: Fresh, in-flower plants delivered consistently throughout the season. Many retailers complain that growers flower the entire lot of a particular crop, sell out, and then have no more. Consequently, if a particular variety flowers somewhat early, retailers find themselves in a bind when that same variety flowers in the natural landscape (which serves as a giant billboard) and they're unable to get plants.

The Future of Retail Display

No other area of the garden center retail display is undergoing such a radical transformation as perennials. While it's true that consumers recognize the word perennial and have increased knowledge of what the term means because of heightened media coverage, most retailers will tell you that consumers simply want flowers.

Consider these facts: From industry research, we know that sales of most common bedding plants are basically flat. The industry is growing because as a whole we're selling more diverse product to customers. Now, add to that Martha Stewart's promotion of unusual plants—especially perennials—and ask yourself, "Is it any surprise that perennials are booming?" After all, they aren't the same boring impatiens, petunias, and marigolds that have decorated the front of the house for years. It's this overwhelming category diversity that perennials offer that's transforming the retail garden display area into a reflection of consumers' lifestyles: A place where they choose plants to express their individuality and style.

Savvy retailers have jumped on this, banning the strict tree, shrub, perennial, and annual display areas and mixing them together. While some of these trendy retailers may keep a limited selection of perennials displayed in an A-to-Z fashion throughout the season, they're much more likely to throw shrubs, annuals, and perennials side-by-side. This is horticultural blasphemy to many "traditional" growers and retailers who draw strict lines of demarcation between annuals and perennials by having separate buyers and insisting on separate display areas. But it is the future.

Etera—with their branded coco pots, fabulous information-packed pot wraps and tags, and colorful kiosks—is also helping to break the perennial A-to-Z display mold. For the Etera brand to work, it's got to be out front. Many of the retailers they're working with put the Etera display right up front in the stores, where they draw attention and move product.

Hot Plants

Want a short list of some really hot plants based on our conversations with growers and retailers? This year's hosta buzz is being caused by 'Tattoo', which is available in such limited quantities that it will take several years before enough young plants have been grown for it to show up in any significant quantities in the commercial market.

Ornamental grasses, because of their texture, simplicity, and ease to grow, are still hot, as are hardy tropicals such as gingers and *Heliconia* in southern regions. While most think of hydrangeas as shrubs, they're one of the hottest plants going right now—just take a look at any consumer book, magazine, or home interiors show. *Helleborus,* with their distinctly botanical look and late winter/early spring flowers, are trendy, as is just about any type of lavender or rosemary. Probably one of the absolute hottest trends nationwide are perennials grown for their interesting foliage. Hostas, of course, are the leading seller in this category, but plants like *Heuchera, Pulmonaria,* and *Tiarella* are growing fast. New varieties of these genera are spurring sales. And more on lavender: It's hot for it's foliage and scent, and is absolutely, hands down, the No. 1 selling perennial in Europe right now.

Speaking of Europe, *Gaultheria* and *Skimmia* (popular for fall sales in Europe at the moment) may be considered to be shrubs by some and tender perennials by others, but they offer consumers fabulous berries in the late fall—just the right touch of color for holiday sales and an entirely different look than traditional poinsettias. But both plants have long crop times and are difficult to grow.

Go ahead and make your plans to produce the Perennial Plant Association's Plant of the Year for 2001: *Calamagrostis* x *acutiflora* 'Karl Foerster', an ornamental grass commonly known as feather reed grass. Everyone we asked about the PPA Plant of the Year promotion says it's effective.

No-Brainer Ways to Win with Perennials

How can you just about guarantee success with perennials right now? Here are a few tips:

1. Ship on carts. No one has time to unload stacked plants anymore.
2. Get rid of black-and-white stick plant stakes and only use full-color tags that will help your retailers sell plants even when they're not in bloom.
3. Stage production into the marketplace. After all, your retail customers have limited display space. Are you going to fill that limited space up with color that will walk or with green plants that have less appeal?
4. Try 2- and 3-gal. production for late June, July, and August sales to retailers and landscapers.
5. Expand your pansy and garden mum sales by adding perennials and Fall Magic plants.
6. Produce perennials for spring sales only in covered greenhouses: You'll reduce your overwintering losses and have more control over when plants are put into the market.
7. If you grow only the leading bread-and-butter perennials, you'll have a lot of competition. Staging flowering plants of mainstays and offering them for extended periods will reduce competition, as most growers will be putting green plants into the market except during the natural flowering season.
8. Prebook your young plant orders. Take the initiative to stay in contact with your supplier so that you know about shorts and CNS (cannot supply) before anyone else. Prebooking orders also allows you to get new and special varieties. Waiting until availabilities are released will limit your plant selection to what has already been produced. Many garden centers decide where to purchase their bread-and-butter items based on where they are able to get unusual things.

Big into "Zone Denial"
Skagit Gardens
Mt. Vernon, Washington

At Skagit Gardens, flowers are flowers. Their focus is to get great plants and get them into programs, without worrying over "annual" and "perennial" labels. "Does the plant satisfy someone's needs?" asks Mike Poynter, general manager. "Gaura in 3-in. pots for use as a basket filler, for example? The fact that *Gaura lindheimeri* 'Siskiyou Pink' is a perennial doesn't matter."

Mike says Skagit is big on what they call zone denial. "We give our customers information, but many of the books [about perennials] may not be totally representative of what a plant will do. There's too much emphasis on zones; we forget they're simply plants," he says. Skagit's mantra: Let the consumer make the choice, but give them a choice.

Skagit Gardens grows bedding plants, cool crops, and perennials at two production sites covering forty-nine acres. Three-quarters of the business is finished production to garden centers, Mike says. Currently, Skagit finishes some 3.5 million perennials in 4-in. and 1-gal. pots, most sold in the Puget Sound area.

Mike Poynter shows off Skagit Gardens' newest greenhouse: A 36-ft. Cravo retractable-roof house. The wider span means less steel—and lower cost. This house ran about $10/sq. ft. with Radiant infrared heat, robotic irrigation booms, concrete aisles, gravel bays and roll-up sidewalls.

In 1977, about a third of Skagit's sales were to one chain store, Mike recalls. Today their largest customer has less than 2% of their sales. "When you cater to independents, you never do large runs of anything. But by choosing independent garden centers, we've got a tremendous amount of loyalty. If one dropped us, no problem. The disadvantage is they want a huge selection to set them apart."

For five months of the year, young plants, including perennials, are 90% of their sales. Skagit likes to offer new and exciting items to the trade, such as *Coreopsis* 'Flying Saucers'. But while new perennials are introduced every year, as a group they haven't had the same kind of breeding emphasis as annuals, for several reasons. First, most perennials are "weeds, just species—they're wild," Mike says. "They don't display the good breeding of a *Scabiosa* 'Pink Mist' or 'Butterfly Blue'." Second, there are so many of them. And third, breeding is a slow, laborious process. We talk about perennials like they're a crop, and they're not," Mike says. "They're more different from one another than a petunia and impatiens. A lot of that has to do with breeding."

And You Thought Refrigerators Were for Milk
Carolina Nurseries
Moncks Corner, South Carolina

Speechless is the best way to describe how you feel walking into a cooler capable of holding more than thirty tractor loads of perennials. Carolina Nurseries is using that cooler to stage product into the marketplace. Plants can be held stacked on pallets in the cooler at or just above freezing for up to nine months. When it's time for finishing, the pallets are taken out to the fields by forklift.

While not every grower has the capital base to put in such a cooler, owner J. Guy sees the cooler as just one part of a multipronged approach to being unique in the marketplace. Not to mention the competitive advantage they enjoy at getting plants into the market in color at the right time, which makes him very popular with customers.

Anyone who knows J. knows that once he decides to try something, it's never done in a small way. He'll dive into a new crop with 10,000 units at once. Carolina Nurseries' perennial production exceeds one million units per year in primarily true-gallon sizes among 300 types of plants. They also have an active new-crops development program, headed by Linda Erdman. They're screening some 1,200 perennials and shrubs as possibilities to add to the production mix.

Working in conjunction with the Horticultural Research Institute, Carolina Nurseries is one of the few nurseries actively working to mechanize their production lines. This spring, they were testing a prototype Bouldin & Lawson transplanter designed for nursery stock. They're working on an inventory system that will log plants into a tracking program as soon as they're planted, and they've also invested in 1200 dpi printers to create customized signs and posters for their customers.

Mainstreaming the Esoteric and Unusual
Terra Nova
Canby, Oregon

Pulmonaria, Heuchera, Tiarella, Saxifraga, Tricyrtis—these aren't the top-selling perennials . . . not yet, that is. With creative plant breeding and selection, rapid stock increase through tissue culture, and quick finishing times for final producers, they may soon be leaders. And not only will these plants flower, but their foliage creates all-season interest and expands their sales window from just a couple of weeks to whenever consumers are shopping. It's a clever, planned approach.

Terra Nova's main greenhouse for plant selection and breeding. Currently, they are looking at between fifty and sixty genera.

Terra Nova is one of the only companies in the world that's actively breeding perennials. The nerve center of their research and development is a 3,000-sq. ft. greenhouse filled with hundreds of collected plants that serve as the inspiration for developing new varieties. Terra Nova's target: Martha Stewart types and plant connoisseurs, and people who have been to The Home Depot and are ready for something more.

Their main product is Stage 4 tissue culture liners that finish for growers in eight to ten weeks, or Stage 3 tissue culture plantlets. Propagation greenhouses are equipped with HID lighting to keep plants actively growing, an important point during the short days of winter, since plants have been exposed to light their entire lives in the test tube. Terra Nova's six-hood lab does contract production in addition to multiplying plants for their own sales. Plants go out FedEx second-day air worldwide.

Their main breeding criteria are "Is it interesting, and will it sell?" says Gary Gossett in New Product Development. "Usually you can figure out how to market it if it's interesting for the gardening public."

The ability to produce tissue-culture plants has allowed Terra Nova to get new products into the marketplace quickly. The result is transform-

Some plants are studied for several years outdoors prior to release. In addition to studying performance under Oregon conditions, Terra Nova works with six botanical gardens and universities in the U.S. and Canada.

ing the upper end of the marketplace, Gary says. This rapid increase of supply, combined with rapidly disseminating information directly to retailers and consumers over the Internet, means what used to take thirty years can now happen in just two.

America's Up-and-Coming Supplier
North Creek Nurseries
Landenberg, Pennsylvania

Gather a dozen perennial growers together and ask them about young plant suppliers, and one nursery will be mentioned over and over again: North Creek. Dale Hendricks (well-known in perennial circles) and partner Steve Castorani operate four acres of cover and three to four acres of field in Landenberg and Oxford, Pennsylvania.

Their specialty is bringing the unusual to the wholesale trade. Dale networks his contacts around the globe in search of new plants. North Creek often has items before they're available any place else. That's why some of the East Coast's leading perennial growers buy from them. North Creek also works with mail-order businesses such as Burpee, Spring Hill, and Wayside. Expected liner production volume in 2000 is more than 5 million.

The other facet of their business is in supplying plants for land reclamation and restoration. Their 36-cell Eco-plug can be direct-planted into the landscape by highway departments.

Reliable supply of liners is one of the factors that has helped stoke the perennial fire in the past few years, especially in getting new items into the marketplace. For example, *Eupatorium rugosum* 'Chocolate' "within two years went from obscurity to the mass markets in

Part of North Creek's liner production in Oxford, Pennsylvania.

the tens of thousands," Steve explains. 'Chocolate' was able to ascend so fast because it can be rapidly produced as a liner.

In the last months, North Creek has refocused their mission statement. "We want plants that are sustainable in the landscape," Steve says. "They have to hold up to certain criteria: require little or no chemicals for pest control and be noninvasive." For instance, they got out of *Miscanthus* a long time ago because it tends to be invasive. Instead, they pushed noninvasive alternatives, such as *Panicum virgatum*, that have a similar growth habit and form.

Reliable supply is also essential. "It's one thing to have cool plants," Steve says, "but if we can't get it into production, why bother?"

Supplying Growers with Variety
Blooming Nursery
Cornelius, Oregon

Like most perennial growers, Grace Dinsdale has a wide selection—some 1,400 different items. Also like most perennial growers, Grace makes the bulk of her sales from a leading few. "It's the 80/20 rule," Grace says. So why not focus on just the 20% generating all the volume? "We can't do that," she replies. "Who we are is the 80% that makes it worthwhile for people to buy from us," a statement especially true of Blooming Nursery's liner business.

Blooming Nursery decided to pursue liner sales nine years ago, dropping the retail side of the operation. Today, business is about evenly split between liners and finished plants.

The perennial liner market moves fast, Grace says. About 20 to 25% of their liner sales are custom grown; the remainder of their production is grown on speculation. "There are so many variables," Grace says. "We work far enough in advance so that the crop is established when the customer has given us enough lead time." While twelve weeks is their average liner production time, some plants may take five to six months to produce prior to being sold. "I'm not proud of our crop turns, but I'm proud of the quality. I don't believe you can have both."

Liner production is in 50-count or 36-count bottomless pots. Grace says they went to the bottomless pot because it grows the best liner. Drainage is good, they hold longer, and are easier to dislodge.

Overall, about 60,000 sq. ft. of the nursery's total 250,000-sq. ft. covered area is devoted to liner production. For both liners and finished production, Grace uses Cravo retractable-roof greenhouses. Flood floors help keep foliage dry. Half are concrete, but Grace is also using heavy plastic pond liner to create waterproof bays. To increase air under the roots, they added a screen that breaks the water column. Outdoor production area includes twenty-five acres of field stock and bareroot perennial production.

Blooming Nursery switched to bottomless pots for their young plant sales because they grow better plants, owner Grace Dinsdale says. In the photo, a 36-count *Achillea* plug.

Most finished production is in 3½-in. pots wholesaling for $1.15, but "it needs to be $1.25," Grace admits. For two years, Blooming Nursery has been working with a true 4-in. pot selling for $2.25 to $2.75 as a way to supply a larger plant with a better shelf life and to distinguish their product in the marketplace. But Grace can't risk dropping 3½-in. pots yet because the Portland market is hooked on them. However, the larger, true 4-in. pots can retail under $5, so long-term it should be a good size. "If [a plant is] below $5, people don't have to think about it before they buy—it's an impulse purchase," she says.

Branding a Unique Product
Etera
Mt. Vernon, Washington

Etera's bottomless coco pot is cleverly packaged: Perennials are divided into eight groups such as hostas, groundcovers, daylilies, etc. Each type gets its own hex box packaging, with each specific variety getting its own storybook tag. Not only do plants have a tag, but there's enough copy with each plant to give even the most timid gardener enough information to be successful. Garden center dealers can purchase a matching wooden kiosk that displays plants and plant information, the Etera catalog, and garden guide. The cost is rebated to the dealers from sales made from the catalog. Dealers get other benefits such as personalized clothing, signs, handouts and customized Web site development based on their level of purchases. Suggested per-plant retail prices vary from $5.49 to $9.95.

This past spring, nearly a thousand garden centers stocked Etera plants, and Etera also sold direct to home gardeners from their Web site, with local dealers—selected by consumers from a list on the site—getting 15% of the transaction. "We ship to the consumer, and we send a commission to the garden center. The more we support the model, the more business we'll get," says Roger Heins, senior vice president of marketing.

At the heart of the Etera perennial is the EteraPlug—a field-grown perennial in a 3-in. bottomless pot. Perennial plants are dug from some three hundred acres of fields, cutting off feeder roots. Plants are stored in the freezer until they're needed for potting in the winter or spring. Once potted, they'll go into the warm propagation house to initiate rooting in and later moved to a cool house or a Cravo retractable-roof house for finishing and holding. "The key is using bottom heat for roots and a cool or cold environment for shoots," says John Walden, director of production. Some 350 different items are available as Etera perennials.

An aggressive new product development program keeps new plants moving into the program. In 2000, some eighty-three new plants were added, while twenty were dropped. "We see the garden center business increasing, and we see perennials being the leader," Roger forecasts.

Focus on the Unusual, and Customers Will Come
Messenbrink's Nursery & Perennials
Nashville, North Carolina

"We were told we'd have a difficult time selling the unusual, but we decided to go with them anyway, and we've ended up being more successful," Mark Messenbrink says of his business's focus. Nine years after that decision, Mark says demand for his product is "up, up, up. We can't meet the demand." Plants such as variegated *Alstroemeria, Cyclamen hederifolium, Danaë racemosa, Hippeastrum* 'San Antonio Rose', *Polygonatum,* and *Smilax* are Messenbrink's calling cards.

While the unusual items draw customers to Messenbrink's, it's the bread-and-butter plants that form the bulk of their sales. Their two leading sellers are *Verbena* 'Homestead Purple' and *Lantana* 'Miss Huff'.

Most of their production is sold green, and they're known for their 1-gal. hexagonal pots. Production volume averages 200,000 units a year from four acres. Most plants are potted in late summer or early fall. For vigorous varieties like *Achillea,* they'll hold them in 24-cell packs and then plant into larger pots in the winter.

Mark's concerns for the future of perennials center around overproduction of commodity items. "Demand exists, but I don't know how quickly the market will be flooded." While larger nurseries are taking market share in fast-moving items like 'Homestead Purple' or 'Miss Huff', Mark sees that he must continue to focus on smaller volume, slow-growing plants to maintain his market niche.

June 2000

Raising the Bar
Jennifer Duffield White

When you hear mass merchants and plants in the same sentence, you'll likely imagine a grower grumbling about the yellowing mass of leaves left to bake in the parking lot. But there are always exceptions to standard perceptions, people who know what it takes to leave mediocrity in the dust, with flair. Hampshire Farms of Hampshire, Illinois, is one such example.

You don't meet too many perennial growers who jump into business with the sole intention of just serving a few big chains. But Hampshire Farms did just that four years ago, and they rapidly proved their case for quality, distribution, and a focus on the end-consumer.

We'd heard good words circulating the Midwest about Hampshire Farms (formerly known as Klehm Ornamentals). In fact, they practically sit in *GrowerTalks'* backyard. So we dropped in for a neighborly visit just as spring was clicking into high gear.

When we pulled up one morning in early May, the shipping area had already been swept clean and lines of racks stood green and blooming, waiting to be loaded onto trailers. By the looks of it—gallon containers holding gorgeous perennials with giant Hampshire Farms tags containing more information than most travel brochures—you might have guessed they were headed for an independent garden center. That is, until Hampshire Farms president Sean McDermott tells you they only have three customers: Kmart, Home Depot, and Sears Hardware.

With twelve acres in production and another thirty-eight acres yet to develop, Hampshire Farms has plenty of room to grow. They've already added more office space, with plans in the works to expand their production area.

Sure enough, upon closer inspection, we saw a row of carts with containers holding two tags, one of them being for Kmart's Martha Stewart Everyday Gardening program. And if you sneaked a peek over the shoulder of an employee scanning in the bar codes on each cart, you'd discover shipments destined for stores ranging as far as North Dakota in the west, Ohio in the east, south to St. Louis and Kansas City, and north to the Canadian border.

Jumping for Opportunities

"Trial by fire," is how Sean describes their first year in business, but luck was on their side, as well as a well-designed facility and a plan of attack. It all began when Ron Iverson sold Iverson Perennials to Hines, who moved the operation to South Carolina. Four partners—Kit Klehm; his father, Roy Klehm; John Cusack; and Frank Mariani—realized this created a giant opportunity in perennials, so they joined together to build a company that could supply mass merchants in the Midwest. Originally operating under the name Klehm Ornamentals, they kicked into action, building a facility and business plan worthy of high volume sales, but with an added emphasis on customer service and marketing.

With multiple partners, Hampshire Farms looks to be well rounded from every angle. Sean joined Hampshire Farms shortly after its inception, bringing twelve years of banking experience with him, which, he says, brings in a different perspective whenever they're analyzing new opportunities and future plans. Frank also owns Mariani Landscape in Lake Bluff, Illinois, and Mariani Nursery in Kenosha, Wisconsin. He contributes a wealth of business and industry experience. And to round things out, John, a private investor, adds his own business sense to the mix.

Sean, John, and Frank bought out the Klehms last fall and changed the name to Hampshire Farms, with the hopes of developing brand-name recognition at the consumer level. The Klehms still own Song Sparrow Perennial Farm in Avalon, Wisconsin, which supplies Hampshire Farms with many of its daylilies.

Designed for Speed

Distribution, distribution, distribution. Let's put it this way: Hampshire Farms has received a U.S. process patent for the manner in which they handle the plants in their greenhouse.

These poppies are a specialty crop, headed to add a splash of color at Home Depot stores.

"You have to understand what's important to the chains because it's different than what's important to the independents," says Sean. Part of that is meeting the challenge of distribution. They can ship to up to five hundred stores in a given week. But it also means getting on the phone and getting plants in color out on the sales floor—even if they're a week ahead of schedule.

They designed Hampshire Farms from the get-go for efficient product and labor movement. They buy in all their perennials as plugs, bareroots, and young plants, and pot them up and finish them off on their twelve-acre production area. Certain varieties are brought in during the fall and overwintered, mostly in gutter-connected greenhouses, although they also have individual Quonsets. Others, like the daylilies, overwinter outdoors on the ground between the Quonsets. The large, gutter-connected facility with a vented roof from Paul Boers is primarily used for hosta production.

Everywhere you walk at Hampshire Farms, you encounter Dutch trays: not for growing, but for transportation. The rail system crisscrosses the entire twelve acres, running into the Quonsets and in-between them as well. Sean explains that it makes pulling plants for shipment fast and efficient, especially since they have more than five hundred varieties.

Tags like these are firmly fastened to every pot that leaves Hampshire Farms. The tags, manufactured by Horticultural Printers, serve as a way to connect with consumers, says Sean. Easy-to-read symbols on the front denote the plant's requirement for full sun. The "N" means it's native to the U.S. and the butterfly symbol makes it easy for both customers and employees to pick out butterfly attractants. On the reverse side, you'll find complete descriptions of the variety—from height, to hardiness, to where it should be planted, with detailed care instructions.

Once the perennials are placed in six-pack carrying trays on the benches, they're rolled to the central conveyor line near the loading docks, where they're tagged and put on racks. Each shipping cart has a bar code, which is scanned into the computer system so they know which store it's heading to. In addition, every rack has its own little "map" that tells the rack loaders which variety goes on each shelf.

From there, Hampshire Farms depends on top-notch truck drivers, whom they hire as independent contractors, to represent the company. "It's really important that we control the trucking," says Sean, explaining that their drivers self-unload when they arrive at the stores. It saves time and lets them plan more accurately because they never have to wait three hours for the chains' employees to unload for them. Plus, Sean says the drivers are one of the most important links to the stores, sometimes spending as much time each week with the store contacts as nearly anyone else in the company. And for added incentive: Drivers get paid for each rack they bring back.

Serenading the Chains

If there's a single secret in dealing with the chains, it's that each store needs individual attention. In fact, Sean advises that if you're interested in serving the mass market, you really need to do your own market studies of the stores and areas you'd be serving. Ask yourself, what has to happen at the stores in order for you to be successful?

"You have to focus less on what you want and more on what'll be interesting to the people who buy your plants," advises Sean, particularly if you're interested in selling volume. At Hampshire Farms, they find themselves focusing more and more on the end consumer and marketing. They spend a lot of their time talking to the stores and getting feedback from managers and actual customers. Currently, they're in the process of setting up a Web site, www.hampshirefarms.com, that they hope will strengthen feedback. But the top priority on their list right now is to keep bringing in new varieties.

"They all present different challenges," says Sean of the chains, stressing that each store has a different personality. While you have to develop relationships with buyers, there's also a serious need to develop relationships at the store level. "It has an impact on how your plants are merchandized and sold." While they don't officially run a merchandising program, Sean says, "we will put people in stores to merchandise . . . if we see an opportunity to make our plants more attractive and sell more."

Hampshire Farms may have an advantage over older businesses in that they were physically built to serve the mass market, but they also have a management team that's not afraid to think progressively as they approach their customers. In fact, Sean says they're not opposed to moving beyond their current customer base. "Over time we hope to develop a way to serve independent garden centers in an efficient manner."

But the chains still look promising for Hampshire Farms. "As the chains continue to grow, they'll continue to be a lot of opportunities out there," explains Sean. With fifty acres of property and only twelve in production so far, there's plenty of room, and Hampshire Farms is already looking towards an expansion.

Quality off the Bench

Let's face it, quality isn't exactly synonymous with the plants you find in chains. But Sean attributes much of their success to the high caliber plants they strive to produce. For Hampshire Farms, quality is key in moving their product.

Think of it this way: You can't always depend on having expert staff at the chains who'll take care of your plants once they arrive. "If it doesn't sell real quickly," admits Sean, "you've got a problem." But on the same note, "If it's really nice stuff, it's going to sell." Mass merchants offer a constant stream of customers through their stores. Thus, if you concentrate on delivering good-looking perennials, mostly in bloom, then they'll move quickly. And you won't need to worry about their condition deteriorating as they sit in the store.

On the growing side of things, Production Manager Joe Smolecki has his job cut out for him: scheduling hundreds of varieties, in both large and small quantities. Joe says that requires "continually adjusting the starter plant size, growing environment, soil mix, and cultural practices. We're trying to stay abreast of all the new research that has been coming out on perfecting perennial production."

Along with always trying to upgrade and expand their offering of the tried-and-true favorites, they're always out for items that catch the customer's eye. Offerings like *Viola* 'Purple Showers', *Dianthus* 'Tiny Rubies', and what Joe calls "the somewhat bizarre *Juncus* 'Spiralis'." However, Joe notes, "We're also trying to familiarize the public with less well-known but still dependable-performing perennials such as *Heuchera, Tiarella,* and *Pulmonaria.*" But all new candidates undergo a rigorous set of height, hardiness and ease-of-culture specifications.

Process Patent?

We've heard of plant patents, but we've never walked into a greenhouse and learned that the way they handle their plants is patented.

So we were a little surprised and perplexed to learn that Hampshire Farms has a U.S. process patent. When they built their facility from the ground up a few years ago, the partners at Hampshire Farms worked real hard to streamline everything—from the straight rows to the Dutch tray rail system to the way each part of their facility is connected. "A lot of growers have structures all over the place," explains Sean, noting that these growers have expanded slowly, over many years.

The owners at Hampshire Farms knew they had a novel setup, and an attorney suggested they patent it. But we're not just talking about just the efficient layout. It includes the whole process: The way they pick plants off the floor, put them in six-pack holding trays, onto Dutch benches, roll them to the shipping area, tag the pots on a conveyor line, and place them on the racks.

Perhaps it's a little bizarre—the idea even makes Sean laugh a bit. But, he says, "It was unique enough that we wanted to have a say if anyone wanted to copy it exactly."

June 2001

The Reinvention of Bluemount Nurseries

Chris Beytes

A nursery built almost exclusively on a love of plants will find the going pretty rocky in today's harsh business climate. That was the reality facing long-time perennial specialist Bluemount Nurseries.

Run for many years by Richard Simon, one of the true legends and pioneers in America's perennial industry, Bluemount is today in the hands of the third generation, Richard's daughter, Martha, and her husband, Nick Pindale. Their goal was finding the formula that blends

Bluemount's tradition of quality, excellence, and innovation with modern business practices borrowed straight from corporate America. And with a five-year plan on track that will increase sales fivefold, the formula is obviously working.

Perennial Pioneers

Based in the small northern Maryland town of Monkton, Bluemount was founded in 1926 by Andrew and Katherine Simon, who moved their landscaping and perennial business from Towson, Maryland, to the current Blue Mount Road site in the late 1940s. Their son, Richard, took over the business after graduating from Cornell University and spending time working at several of Europe's premier gardens, such as Kew and Wisley.

The business remained small and continued to grow perennials. However, it began to expand into bamboo and ornamental grasses, even though those crops weren't yet the darlings of the industry. "My father and grandfather were true plant nuts," says Martha. "They weren't out to make a lot of money; they just loved plants and loved the business."

As perennials grew in popularity, Bluemount's reputation expanded. In perennial circles, Bluemount was a Mecca in the U.S. Even notable English horticulturist and perennial specialist Adrian Bloom worked at Bluemount when he was in his early twenties. Kurt Bluemel, owner of well-known perennial nursery Kurt Bluemel Inc., Baldwin, Maryland, came to the U.S. from Germany in the 1960s at Andrew and Richard's invitation to work at Bluemount.

Richard also put Bluemount at the front of the perennial industry when he became actively involved with the fledgling Perennial Plant Association in 1984 as a director and later as the association's third president.

Competition Heats Up

With such a world-renowned reputation in perennials, you'd think Bluemount's success and longevity would be guaranteed. The business had built to $800,000 in sales, and Richard's son, Dan, and daughter, Martha, had both joined the business. But increased competition (often from the very growers Richard helped put into the perennial business), growing production costs, and aging, inefficient facilities combined to cut heavily into Bluemount's profits. It was obvious that an outside point of view was needed to bring some fresh business ideas to Bluemount. Recalls Martha: "We felt like we were at a crossroads: The company was either going to have to get a lot bigger or stay small, and we were going to have to get a lot more efficient or lose our shirts."

Another problem, says Nick Pindale, was that their bank was nervous that Bluemount's leaders didn't know their unit costs and didn't seem to have any idea about what costs went into their products. "They were asking the typical questions that banks ask," he says, "and nobody knew the answers."

The outside view came from consultant Robert Hayter, who made some fundamental belt-tightening recommendations. He also talked to Martha and Nick about how they saw themselves fitting into the business. Nick (who was helping out at Bluemount in his spare time) was on the fast track to assistant manager at the Federal Reserve. With a degree in personnel and industrial relations, he imagined a lucrative career with the Federal Reserve Bank, an early retirement, and only then coming into the nursery business full time.

Meanwhile, Martha was following in her father's footsteps as a perennial specialist. Like Richard, she spent several years working at perennial nurseries in Europe, doing internships at Blooms of Bressingham in England, as well as at nurseries in Holland, Germany, and the U.S. While she knew her role a Bluemount would expand as her knowledge increased (she had already taken over as propagator and updated their techniques), she never gave any thought to actually running the company. But that would soon change.

"I remember Robert Hayter sitting me down at the picnic table out in our shade area," she says. "He said he'd talked with all of our employees, and he felt that it was time for Dan and Nick and I to get much more involved in the leadership of the nursery. I was just so floored because I'd never thought about it. Me? My dad had been running the business forever . . . he was the guru and the god, and everybody loved him and worshipped him. I never thought that he would ever step down."

And what did Richard think about the proposed changes? "He was really excited and open-minded about the future," Martha says. "He realized that Dan and I were adults and needed to have a living. We'd talked about subdividing the land and eventually building houses. (Both built houses on the property—Dan has since left the business and relocated.) So he was starting to realize that the nursery was going to have to start providing for more than just him and my mom."

"He actually started the ball rolling," says Nick of Richard's push to modernize the business. "I think it just grew too quickly. The growth wasn't planned. Sales were driving the growth, and then the bills were driving the growth, because they still weren't concentrating on the bottom line."

Looking Toward $5 Million

The past four years have seen a major explosion of growth for Bluemount, with a new propagation facility and ten new greenhouses. To turn the business from slowly sinking to expanding and profitable took a major overhaul in the way Bluemount was run, including a five-year plan, a new management structure, and the implementation of modern accounting practices and Standard Operating Procedures.

The target for the company's growth came from a formal business plan. "It was three years ago that we actually sat down and put together three- and five-year plans," Nick says. Their plan was to reach $2.5 million after three years and $5 million in five years.

"Richard thought we were nuts thinking that we could sell $2 million a year in perennials," Nick recalls. "I think at that time [1995] we were at $900,000." He says Bluemount's expenses had been growing, but sales were almost flat. They weren't increasing inventory at a rate that would let them keep up with the level of debt they were incurring for capital improvements.

The long-range plans targeted an economy of scale based on their fixed operating expenses and debt load. Now, when they put up a $3,000 greenhouse, they know it will turn over $30,000 worth of plants a couple of times a year, Nick says.

So far, the three-year portion of the plan is right on target. They left 1998 as a year of evaluation to see how realistic their goals are and to tweak the plan if necessary. With their production expense challenges mostly solved, the biggest hurdle is financing. "We can't continue to fund growth out of our operating expense—and we only have eighty acres that we own," Nick says. "Our biggest asset is the inventory, and nobody wants to let us use that as collateral. So we're sitting on millions of dollars worth of inventory that's worth nothing to the bank."

Seeing this as an industry wide problem, Bluemount began working with the Maryland Nurserymen's Association on programs to educate Maryland bankers about the nursery industry and encourage them to become partners in the growth of Maryland's second largest agricultural commodity. One result of their effort is that bankers who once turned them away are now looking for Bluemount's business.

Addressing the Labor Challenge

Under the old Bluemount management structure, Richard sat at the top, with Martha, Nick, and Dan below him, and the remaining thirty-five or so employees in various departments made up the company. Few people had any authority. Decisions were made in family meetings on a day-to-day basis.

Richard officially retired in 1996 (he and his wife, Janet, are now volunteer resident grandparents at a Quaker boarding school in Ohio). The structure was changed in 1998 both to expand ownership in the company and to expand employee responsibilities. Martha was named president and Nick was named CFO. Under them are three key employees: George Mayo, head of sales and administrative affairs; Tim Cranston, in charge of nursery operations; and Ross Patterson, production manager. Ross has three growers under him, one per section, and also handles field production and potting. Tim has been instrumental in all the new construction at the nursery.

The new structure decentralizes the authority and gives department heads more of a role as company managers. It also gives actual ownership to key employees such as George and Tim, who now own stock shares.

"It has made all the difference in morale and excitement," Martha says. For instance, Tim has worked for Bluemount for fifteen years and has always called himself a "lifer." "But now, since we gave him ownership, he's a maniac!" says Martha. "All these ideas!"

Nick says that kind of employee involvement and dedication is essential for the rapid growth curve they're experiencing. Martha can be out lecturing or finding new varieties while Nick is getting more involved in the political side of the industry and the company will keep running. "A good leader makes himself or herself obsolete," Nick says. "If we're not on the property, the whole place doesn't grind to a halt."

Nick the Watchdog

An integral part of Bluemount's reinvention is a strong focus on the bottom line through accurate activity-based cost accounting, courtesy of Nick and his experience with the Federal Reserve. Before, they simply lumped all production costs together and put them against the end products, rather than knowing what each stage of production cost. But activity-based accounting let them see the difference in what they were paying for cuttings versus what it would cost to do them themselves, Nick says.

"How much is it costing us to produce a plug?" he asked. "What does the average plug cost to buy in? Wow, look at the difference! We can do it a lot cheaper. That was the justification to really beef up propagation." At that time, Bluemount could grow a plug for 28% cheaper than to buy one in. "We've since gotten it down to 51% cheaper per plug to produce them ourselves," says Nick.

They've also started paying more attention to costs of the plant material they buy in, especially for such things as shipping charges. Nick says they'd sometimes spend $2.00 before adding labor to grow a plant that they'd sell for $1.75. While Martha calls Nick "a closet plant maniac" (he's responsible for the massive display gardens around their house), when it comes to the nursery, he questions every expense and digs to find ways to cut costs. For instance, cutting out the middleman when it comes to vendors and cooperative buying, which saves on shipping.

One new tool that helps Nick and Bluemount track their production costs and schedules is their Nursery Wizard management software, developed by GE Capital Consulting with Nick's input (*GrowerTalks*, April 1998, p. 36). He had tried several commercial nursery software packages but couldn't find one that did what Bluemount needed, so he worked with GE to create one that fit the business. GE is now marketing the resulting program.

Still, maintaining a list that's 1,200 to 1,400 varieties long is tough for any nursery to justify. Says George Mayo: "If this business seriously wanted to be strictly a profit-making business, it would cut down to 250 varieties."

Martha says she has battles over the size of their list—with herself, with the growers, with everybody. And every year they add more varieties—over a hundred in 1997 and over eighty this year. "And we dropped, what, ten?" asked Nick. "We probably make money on about four hundred of those varieties."

So how does he justify that against his accounting system? "I justify it because that's our niche," he answers. "That's what Bluemount is known for—having the new varieties—with a lot of the newer varieties you don't want to rush into doing 3,000 in production because they're not yet tested. Some growers do, but our philosophy has been not to do it." The Pindales plant out a new variety in their garden for a year to test it, then put a few hundred into production the first year. Those small volumes are costly, but the company feels it pays in the long run to do them, to be able to ensure the customer gets a quality plant that will perform.

"We've gotten a few new customers this year because they know that we have such a large selection and their customers are demanding more varieties," says George.

Consistency in an Inconsistent World

Another new management tool that will help bring Bluemount into the twenty-first century is Standard Operating Procedures, or SOPs. Nick explains: "The reason Bluemount has such a strong customer base right now—over 1,700 customers in the files—is that we make everything as uniform and consistent as possible. We understand that retailers' space is as valuable as grocers' shelves. Anything they put on their tables has to move as quickly as possible."

SOPs help Bluemount achieve uniformity and consistency with noto-riously inconsistent peren-nials by standardizing all of the regular plant production chores—every-thing is potted, watered, pinched, and maintained in the same way. For instance, propagators are trained to "not stick the junk." Instead, they learn to grade cuttings carefully for uniform trays. Uniform cuttings yield uniform finished plants.

Martha Simon Pindale checks the root development of a 1-qt. perennial. Consistency of their finished product is a Bluemount hallmark.

And propagation works in conjunction with sales

and production. Before, propagation had no set schedule, resulting in very non-uniform cuttings. Now, young plants are moved out for potting as soon as they're ready and on schedule. "It's had a huge impact on every other stage of growth," says George.

Waterers are trained using a simple tool: baby powder. Martha or the growers will go through the houses ahead of new waterers squirting powder on blocks of plants that need water until new waterers learn to recognize what needs watering.

"One of the reasons for the SOPs is that there's a lot of turnover in this industry," says Nick. "So the faster we can educate people and the more routine we can make some of the operations, the faster they can learn the job."

Realizing the Goal

The reinvention of Bluemount Nurseries is only three years old, and already the results are obvious. They expect to reach their sales goal of 40% over last year's sales without increasing their labor force. As they smooth the bumps out of the basic changes and begin to eye the $5 million mark, they're already implementing more advanced projects, such as branding. They've put together an attractive POP kit and a Web site aimed at consumers (www.bluemount.com) and are doing a small branding project with Maryland retailer Behnke Nurseries featuring "Bluemount's Blue Ribbons."

Martha says her dad was the most modest person you'd every meet, "But we're not very modest," she says of the new Bluemount Nursery.

"It's not that we're not modest," adds Nick, "it's that it's an intricate part of our marketing strategy. To stay alive, we're shouting to the rooftops that we're great; we've been here a long time, and we're going to be here a lot longer."

June 1998

Perennial Precision

Debbie Hamrick

The fact that Louis Stacy spent a full career in the military isn't lost on those who meet him for the first time. As a former navy fighter pilot,

Louis brings a sense of regimen and decorum to even the simplest tasks involved in running a greenhouse business. The nursery appears ready for inspection at all times, with beds immaculately laid out and maintained. Louis and his employees greet one another in a friendly but formal way. From the potting lines to the loading dock, discipline abounds.

Stacy's Greenhouses and Nurseries is one of the Southeast's leading color growers. With three locations covering more than 3 million sq. ft. of growing area—including ten acres of shade houses and 400,000 sq. ft. of greenhouses—the nursery spreads out on three farms just north of York, South Carolina. Their own garden center at the edge of town keeps production rooted in the end result: gardening consumers.

Colorful tractor trailers covered on both sides with a garden scene featuring bright perennials and the Stacy's logo are a regular site on the I-85 corridor between Atlanta, Georgia, and Raleigh, North Carolina, and on the smaller roads in between. The region Stacy's caters to is booming. Like many other parts of the country, unemployment in the Carolinas is 2% or less. New businesses such as BMW's U.S. manufacturing facility and the U.S. headquarters for several of the world's leading pharmaceutical companies and the nation's leading banks have created an economic base of light and heavy manufacturing. High-paying computer, banking, and service jobs contrast the traditional agricultural production in the eastern part of the region. Plus, the Appalachian Mountains are home to some of the country's hottest retirement communities.

When Louis first started in the industry back in 1970, he began as a traditional bedding plant grower. Over time, the nursery transformed into the nation's largest pansy grower (1.5 million flats) and one of the largest perennial growers in the Southeast. That gives them production and marketing niches that fit around the region's bedding plant production giants, which include Metrolina, Baucom's, Van Wingerden International, and Rockwell Farms, all a short distance away in North Carolina. Add oversized 3-by-8-in. custom tags for perennials and specialty annuals, combination pots, and other potted lines that make his product stand out on retailers' shelves, and it's easy to understand Louis's success—and perhaps why so many other growers in the area look to Stacy's as a marketing leader.

The proof is in the pudding: Stacy's sales have increased more than eight-fold since 1994, and "we see no signs of growth abating," Louis says. Plans are to double sales yet again in the next three years.

Perennials Are King

"Our growth [in perennials] is attributed to the fact that we market 90% in full color," Louis says.

Stacy's Greenhouse and Nurseries appears ready for inspection at any time, thanks to owner Louis Stacy's navy-influenced management style.

"Most people who buy, buy it because it's pretty. There aren't a lot of people who know a great deal about what they're buying." Plus, marketing perennials in color taps into consumers' desires. "People want the results of gardening, as opposed to all the work that goes with it."

Stacy's began marketing all perennials in shuttle trays this year. "If you display just the pots, they get jammed together," Louis points out. Not only does product stay fresher and get less shopworn in stores when displayed in trays, but shipping is easier, too.

Like many traditional perennial growers, Stacy's used to get most perennial starter plants in the late summer and fall for planting, over-winter the pots, and sell the plants the following spring. But Louis says that's changing: "We don't do as many [perennials] in the fall as we used to. We've found we can turn many things in six to eight weeks in the spring and make them just as good."

Many bedding plant growers are looking to perennials as a way to boost sales before and after the bedding plant season, but Louis warns that perennials aren't as easy as they look from the outside. "I've seen a lot of bedding growers get into and out of perennials," he says. But persistence can pay: Stacy's own perennial production began in 1988 with 10,000 plants and has grown to 10 million units a year on eighty acres.

Getting into the Stores

In-store merchandising and display support is key to the Stacy's relationship with Lowe's, their leading customer. Stacy's services some 120 Lowe's stores and has installed built-in display fixtures, has developed customized POP signs and posters, and currently employs 130 people full-time throughout the year to service the displays. Three trainers work with these in-store merchandisers.

"Our goal is to sell plants 365 days a year," Louis says. Unlike many traditional retailers, Lowe's, The Home Depot, and other stores in the home center category pull traffic year-round, creating sales opportunities every day. The product assortment shifts through the seasons: Spring is perennials, Proven Winners, and other specialty annuals; summer is specialty annuals and perennials; fall is pansies, perennials, and Fall Magic; and winter is pansies.

In-store merchandisers work in conjunction with Lowe's nursery specialists, but they do not automatically restock shelves. Merchandise is purchased, not shipped, on consignment: Reorders must come from the garden center manager, not one of Stacy's in-store people.

Eight sales reps follow up with buyers several times a week, in addition to faxing daily live inventory availability. Four people are dedicated to keeping track of inventory at three farm locations.

Stacy's also works with Kmart, Pike Family Nurseries in Atlanta, and between 600 and 800 independent garden centers. While most sales are within a 250-mile radius, Stacy's product can be found in fourteen states up and down the eastern seaboard.

Advice to New Growers

"We're a thirty-year overnight success story," Louis jokes. Like most entrepreneurs, the company is Louis, and Louis has held just about every position within the company. "I want everything done exactly as I want it done. . . . Growing is the easiest part; there's a procedure for everything."

Louis puts strong emphasis on staffing. "The rapid growth we've experienced in the last six or seven years wouldn't have been possible without the outstanding management team we've assembled during the last five years." Stacy's employs about 470 people, and Louis is quick to point out that the credit for the nursery's success goes to their employees.

Louis advises new growers to prevent problems rather than waiting for problems to happen. That's a characteristic he's noticed among other successful growers. "Outstanding growers do what they have to do before they have to do it. Average growers wait."

Another piece of advice is to avoid the low-price trap. "'I'll sell for less' is a sure path to destruction. You've got to have a fair price. If we can't make a profit, we're not going to grow it."

But his best advice may be to focus on where you are going. "We don't worry about what other people do; we worry about what we do," Louis says. "As long as we grow beautiful plants, we have no problems selling."

January 2000

Behind the Scenes at Yoder Green Leaf

Debbie Hamrick

The Green Leaf catalog, www.green-leaf-ent.com, is like a bible to many in the perennial business: When growers just can't find it anywhere else, Green Leaf is likely to list it, show a picture, and have a description along with the correct botanical name and variety designation. Their spot availability is almost as extensive. With ten different production locations spanning some forty acres in Pennsylvania, South Carolina, and California, Green Leaf is America's largest perennial supplier and leading perennial specialist. If they don't know the answer, the question may remain unanswered indefinitely.

Mum breeder Yoder Brothers purchased Green Leaf four years ago. Since then, the company has been undergoing deep, structural reorganization in a repositioning to keep it as the leading perennial player for coming decades. Green Leaf customers have been aware of small changes that have emerged in the catalog, product listings, and shipping policies. To get a look at what's going on behind-the-scenes, we visited Green Leaf's new Lancaster production facilities and company headquarters in February. If you're a Green Leaf customer, here's the scoop on their 1½-year-old Lancaster propagation facility. If you buy-in perennial liners from other suppliers, read on, because Green Leaf is in the process of changing the paradigm.

First Things First: BO and CNS

No grower wants to see the words *backordered* (BO) or *cannot supply* (CNS) on order acknowledgments or packing slips. With perennials, the sheer number of different varieties compounds BO and CNS. For Green Leaf, managing 2,100 stock items is a challenge, especially over ten production locations.

How is Green Leaf structuring their core operations to minimize BO and CNS, and still maintain 2,100 SKUs? The short answer is by carefully making capital improvements, streamlining product assortment, and letting each location produce what they do best.

Before getting into the changes Green Leaf has made over the past three years, it's important to take a look at how growers exacerbate the perennial supply issue. Are we our own worst enemies?

As John Bell, Green Leaf's corporate sales and marketing manager, explains, "Forty percent of Green Leaf's orders come within five weeks of shipping. We're hoping to see that change."

If nearly half of all sales come in so close to ship date, who decides which products are going to actually get into the market? The grower? No. Green Leaf does, because they have to plan for the availability. Very, very few plants of any kind can be cycled into a shippable liner within five weeks of receiving an order. In the future, getting orders in early will be the only way growers will be able to access many new items.

When does Green Leaf know about shorts or CNS? About four to six weeks prior to the ship date, Green Leaf takes a yield count. If orders

Green Leaf Lancaster's 30,000-sq. ft. order staging and packaging area can accommodate up to five thousand trays a day.

will be affected, customers are notified at that time. Product that is available is allocated automatically by computer on a first-ordered/first-filled basis. "Orders that come in last are the most exposed," John warns.

Orders are allocated out of inventory two weeks prior to shipping. At that point, "we ship in the high 90s [percent] of the total flats ordered," says Andy Babikow, head of production.

The best way for you to ensure availability is to get orders in early, especially for new items. If you're not sure exactly how much you'll need because your customers haven't placed orders, putting in early base orders and supplementing them off availability is a good way to go.

Changes for the Future

Over the past years, Green Leaf has sold some of its older Pennsylvania production facilities and is in the process of consolidating production in Pennsylvania (Lancaster, headquarters, Homer City, Kennett Square, and Toughkennamon); Pendleton, South Carolina; and Salinas, California.

One of the most important areas Green Leaf has pioneered in recent years is virus screening their stock plants. The process is time consuming and expensive, but "we're dedicated to having clean material," John says. "In the long run, that material will outperform product that has not been tested."

There are two parts to the cleanup. First, all plants are screened for nine different viruses. "No new introductions are made unless they test clean," John says. For example, *Sedum* 'Frosty Morn' is not yet in the Green Leaf catalog because it has to be cleaned up first so that they can create "select" stock that's virus free.

The second part of the program is not only cleaning up stock initially, but also maintaining elite stock and running an ongoing clean stock program. "All the major vegetatively propagated perennials are in the program," Andy adds. Overall, about thirty genera are "in process" of being indexed. The list includes *Achillea, Geranium, Phlox paniculata,* and *Phlox subulata,* for example.

Elite plants from clean stock are maintained domestically in Florida and South Carolina. They serve as the mother plants for stock plants that are shipped to Yoder Green Leaf's individual rooting/production locations.

The new range in Lancaster covers six acres, half of what the site has been zoned for. Thirty-eight Harnois Ovaltech greenhouses connect to a central covered greenhouse that lets workers to pull orders even when it's snowing outside, while still allowing each structure to run a different temperature. Sidewalls roll up for natural ventilation. Houses are networked into an environmental control system by Argus. The site is prepared for another thirty houses.

The propagation area, Harnois greenhouses again, is fitted with a simple but effective benching system—galvanized cattle fence on wood frames that were locally fabricated. Mist lines run the length of rooting benches, and Schaefer HAF fans run overhead for air circulation. A Cravo curtain system provides overhead shade when needed. Fans in the propagation area are Italian, by Val Air. Plastic weather stripping divides the two main houses in propagation so that a warm propagation house can be maintained along with a cooler hardening house. The site has been prepared for an additional two acres of propagation area.

Irrigation is by well water that's pumped into a 70,000-gallon cistern. Most of the media used at Lancaster is Fafard.

Structures do the job with the right technology and flexibility. Costs for the hoop houses ran about $7.50 per ft.; the propagation houses were about $15 per sq. ft., including concrete.

Tags for every plant are available. Shipments go out FedEx second-day air or by truck. Lancaster's 30,000-sq. ft. order staging and packing area can process up to five thousand trays a day at peak. Truck shipping is available for orders of forty trays (one cart) minimum.

Another strategy Green Leaf has pursued is to let each facility produce what it does best. For example, all the *Verbena, Phlox subulata,* and all of Green Leaf's annual plant offerings are done in Pendleton (also where Yoder propagates hardy mums). Other plants are only produced in Salinas, California.

Other changes in internal operations include product standards. Each item is getting its own specification sheet with minimum and maximum standards, photographs, branching standards, and rooting standards. This year trays started going out as a full seventy-two plants rather than seventy, because patchers now fix empties prior to sale.

All of these changes are slowly leading to an entirely new paradigm for perennial liners: staging. "The grower wants a plant that will pop," John says. To accomplish this, Green Leaf divides their product assortment into various groups. Those with cold vernalization requirements go in deep 30 cells; other plants are grown from seed sown in June or, like *Coreopsis* 'Moonbeam', propagated from June cuttings. "Then we spend the time, money, and effort to warehouse those plants to make sure that we have production available year-round."

Perennial Growth

There are three types of perennial producers: traditional perennial growers who focus on perennials, nurserymen, and greenhouse growers. John sees those companies looking at their per-square-foot return on perennials while at the same time providing the extra level of service required in the marketplace as having the best outlook for the future. "The biggest growth is for those growers providing added services," John says. "Who's been the best at providing the service? The guys paying attention to the per-square-foot turn: greenhouse growers."

And to cater to that subset of perennial producers, Yoder Green Leaf is joining forces with The Paul Ecke Ranch's Flower Fields program to offer 103 perennials that have been selected for their superior performance. Growers can order these plants from Ecke, Green Leaf, or Yoder Brothers, and the plants will be shipped with Flower Fields tags that match the entire POP program. Growers will be able to offer a range of annuals and perennials under The Flower Fields banner.

Which begs the question about the "perennial forcing issue." How does John view forcing? "I've changed my opinion on out-of-season flowering," he replies. "Early on, I thought there was a legitimate concern in duping the public into expecting the same thing the following year. But it's not bad to have *Rudbeckia* in the store in color in May. They'll reflower in July and August in the garden," he explains, citing Michigan State University field trials of forced plants. "It provides homeowners the ability to see what the plant and flower color is when they put their garden together."

June 2000

Burlap, Niches, and Ornamental Grasses

Kathy Whitman

For Gary Trucks of Amber Waves Gardens, Benton Harbor, Michigan, following his passion means working with ornamental grasses. Why grasses? "They just struck me," Gary recalls. "I was working for a land-scaper, saw one in his yard, and thought it was the most fascinating thing I'd ever seen."

When Gary began landscaping on his own, he often combined grasses, daylilies, and hostas in his landscapes, and since nobody grew them in his area, he started growing his own. Gary's nursery is located on one of the busiest roads in the county, and his plants soon began attracting attention. "People were stopping and asking if they could buy them, so we started selling retail on Saturdays and Sundays; then on Thursdays, Fridays, Saturdays, and Sunday . . . by the end of the first year, I said, 'I think I see something coming.'" Of course, he was right—ornamental grasses are the rage, and Amber Waves Gardens is in its sixth year as a thriving full-time retail operation.

Amber Waves Gardens sells ornamental grasses, and also hostas, daylilies, and a few other perennials that are good companions to grasses. Gary's plants are all large, landscape-grade material, field grown, dug to order, and balled and burlapped, except for the hostas, which are in containers.

Pick-Your-Own Service

Customers come to the nursery, walk through the fields, and choose the plants they want. Gary or his wife, Sandy, will either dig the plants immediately or mark them for future pickup. Gary notes that "it has a special appeal when they say 'I want that' and you run and get a shovel and burlap." His delighted customers often say things like, "I get to pick my own?" and "You mean I get the whole thing?" Gary explains that in order to survive and be successful, you've got to create a good niche. And letting customers pick out the biggest, best plant they can find in the field is his niche.

Best in the Field

Gary has found that grasses and daylilies perform much better when field grown. "They're rapid growers that fill out containers, and you can't water them enough to keep them looking good in a pot," he explains. "They become a plant in decline. In the ground, nothing restricts them and they become big plants quickly," which, he adds, "is what people seem to want today."

Such large plants can be challenging to handle, but the customers love the large size, and they'll go to great lengths to get them home.

Ready-to-go defines the clientele at Amber Waves Garden, who tend to return again and again. "By selling large plants, the rate of success is probably 99.9%," says Gary. "We don't have people coming back with failures—they come back for more."

Selling plants this way is labor-intensive and time-consuming. Customers sometimes have to wait their turn, but that's no hardship since the nursery is such a beautiful place. The property includes two to three acres of production area, demonstration gardens, and a pond. Gary notes that they have no tags on the plants and no flashy signs: "We keep the commercial aspect out of it." A pleasant, relaxed atmosphere is their goal, and as Gary explains, "We're here to make money, but buying a plant isn't a prerequisite to coming out. We don't strong-arm people to buy—we don't have to."

Amber Waves Gardens is located in a popular vacation area, so they draw customers from throughout the Midwest and from as far away as Vermont, Minnesota, and Missouri. They come for both the plant material and the customer service. "We're here to help the gardening public," says Gary. "We simplify things for the gardener and always try to inform people—I can't stress that enough." The nursery also offers tours to garden clubs and other groups. Gary creates designs for some customers, and he sells to a few landscapers too.

Yearly production includes about 60 different grasses, 24 daylily varieties, and 120 kinds of hostas. They also produce other good companions for the grasses, including *Echinacea, Sedum, Rudbeckia,* and *Perovskia.* Gary and Sandy are constantly evaluating new varieties and are selective about which ones they carry. For example, there are thousands of daylily varieties, so they select a few good ones to stick with, choosing them based on what's best for their area. Several of the grasses and hostas they offer are their own introductions, and Gary is now breeding grasses, hostas, and daylilies.

Seeking a new marketing niche, Amber Waves Gardens began limited mail order sales of bareroot plants last year. Plants are listed in the fall on their Web site (www.amberwavegardens.com) and ship in early April. They limit the numbers of orders so they can send big plants. Gary goal is to have people remember the box when they open it, to say "wow." Gary and Sandy have been pleasantly surprised at the response for mail order and welcome the supplemental winter income.

What started as a curiosity has now turned into a full-fledged business, serving a small but lucrative niche in ornamental grasses and perennials—a niche that satisfies consumer's desire for personal attention and instant gratification.

June 2001

Perennial Creativity

Cathy Whitman

There's nothing simple about the greenhouse business, but Dave and Elaine Green of Green's Gardens & Nursery, Glen Aubrey, New York, have put together an efficient and profitable program for wholesaling perennials. They started the business in 1991 and decided immediately to stick to wholesale because of their excellent location for trucking. They lease their delivery trucks, use ideas from mass merchandisers to improve efficiency, and have worked out production schedules that minimize overwintering.

Production starts February 15, when they start transplanting plugs from 50- or 72-cell trays into 1-qt. containers. Production of quarts this year was 70,000 pots. For this early crop, they focus on about fifty species of early-blooming perennials, including primrose, forget-me-not, *Dianthus, Arabis, Bellis, Sedum,* and lamb's ear. These crops fill the containers nicely, and most have flowers by April 15, when shipping begins. Variety selection is key. Dave explains, "I think about when varieties naturally bloom in the spring, to provide the first color on our customers' benches. Much of our market is ahead of us in season, so things have to be ready by April 15."

In mid-March, Dave and his crew start potting up the gallons, using starting material in 2-in. or larger pots. Dave notes that "the market is really heading that way—buying in larger plants, to finish material quicker." He overwinters as few plants as possible—just hostas, daylilies, and a few plugs—to save labor and cut losses. He adds, "They don't look as fresh as perennials grown in the greenhouse." This allows him to close most of his 27,000-sq. ft. range in the winter. This year he and his crew grew three crops of gallons, totaling 150,000 pots.

Gallons are the best sellers at the retail end. This year, Dave started using shuttle trays that hold six 1-gal. pots. He noticed them at the chain stores, where there's a big emphasis on moving materials around as quickly as possible with the least labor. Pots are arranged so all the picture tags are facing the same way, which makes a nice package for his customers. The trays are quite sturdy and can be reused. He is now using them for all his customers, finding that they're worth the expense because of savings on labor at the greenhouse and at the garden centers.

Dave added hanging baskets to his product line about four years ago and now grows 5,000 annually. He's had good success with Supertunias, which are easy to grow and need minimal heat, and Proven Winner combination baskets. "There's a large market for late-season baskets," Dave says. "Most of ours are shipped after Memorial Day. The market has expanded, and garden centers are looking for fresh baskets even into July."

Garden centers are also looking for unique products, and Dave has developed several using perennial combinations. Perennial hanging baskets are his specialty. The perennial container gardens require special attention to design, since they don't have the same color impact as many annuals. However, like a well-planned perennial border, they provide a succession of flowers as the different plants bloom at different times. At the end of the season, customers can put the plants in their gardens instead of throwing them out. "It's a great way to get in to a new [customer] because it's unique and helps us get our foot in the door," Dave says. He starts with an upright plant in the center, such as *Hemerocallis* 'Stella d'Oro', *Liatris, or Astilbe,* and includes some trailing plants, such as *Lamium, Dianthus,* and other groundcovers. He uses a wide variety of other plants, including some with interesting foliage such as coral bell varieties with dark leaves. In addition to hanging baskets, they're putting perennials in 14-in. decorative bowls and 5-gal. pots.

About 90% of Dave's customers are retail garden centers, located from Boston to Pittsburgh. They include a mix of some large, upscale stores and also many smaller ones, which Dave stresses are very important in his market. Combination planters must be ordered ahead, but nothing else is prebooked. Each week, he checks his inventory and notes which plants are in bloom. He faxes an availability list to his customers, and then they make their choices and fax it back. The arrangement is very convenient for the garden centers, and Dave explains that "this way, customers don't get everything at once in the spring; they just get what's in color." Recently he's begun extending the season by re-wholesaling Christmas trees to his customer base of 180 garden centers.

Dave thinks that the demand for perennials is still on an upward swing, and he plans to make the most of the trend. "We'll get as big as the market will let us. I see every plant, every container that goes out of here. You work so hard for the final product. . . . I want to make sure it's right."

January 2000

Perennials Plus Premiums Equal Success for Sargent's

Cathy Whitman

Variety is the spice of life, and Sargent's Landscape Nursery Inc. in Rochester, Minnesota, is a business with plenty of it. Forrest Sargent offers his customers full lines of annuals, perennials, and nursery items in two garden centers, along with a design-and-build landscape service and a florist shop.

Managing all of this is complex and challenging. So why develop such a diversified business? "It's a people business as well as a plant business," says Forrest. "It's nice for me as an owner to have developed enough of a business to be able to retain good people and delegate to them."

In his area, the market is relatively limited; Forrest describes the city of Rochester as "an island of commerce with country all around." He continues, "To be big enough to retain good people, we can't specialize in just annuals, for example." Sargent's products and services fit many facets of the community, which is dominated by two businesses: the Mayo Clinic and a large IBM plant. Forrest estimates that ten thousand people per day are in town for medical reasons, and they support a thriving service industry that helps his landscape business. Many doctors garden as a hobby and are looking for new and unusual items. "[We grow] bigger, more specialty types of annuals and perennials. We give them the spacing they need to be a premium plant," says Forrest.

"Bigger plants get a better price, and our customers accept that. We don't try to meet the discount competition, but we do meet the independent competition."

Sargent's sells annuals in flats and some in 4½-in. pots, but Forrest says, "Our biggest line, which sets us apart from the competition, is our 5½-in. jumbo square annual color pots." Forrest recalls that they started growing them in the mid-'80s to fill in during the summer and for spring. While many growers offer larger sizes, Sargent's does them early. The pots are just under 1 gal., and they usually plant them with three plugs each. The result is a nice, full blooming plant that fills, even overflows, the pot. "[They're] like the big red apple in the produce department—instant color," says Forrest. "Our customer base likes that. We have a huge number of patio gardeners and people in townhouses." Sargent's sold about 35,000 last year, filled with an assortment of annuals including pansy, viola, celosia, dahlia, dianthus, marigold, salvia, petunia, impatiens, stock, zinnia, and alyssum. About 24,000 sq. ft. of greenhouse space is devoted to annuals.

Perennial Profits

As in many places, perennials are increasing in popularity at Sargent's. "Perennials tie in to the hobbyist. They move them around, search out different colors, and want to have something their neighbor doesn't have," he says. "Perennials are shining as gardening becomes more popular." To satisfy such customers, Sargent's offers about 750 cultivars—nearly 70 of hostas alone. Rochester has a lot of shady areas, and Forrest notes that shade gardening is a big thing, both for annuals and perennials.

Production Manager Paul Pike explains that they grow perennials in unheated hoop houses: "Against the book—but it really does work," he says. Most species are potted in March and April, many into the jumbo square pots, for spring sales. Starting material is about half bareroot divisions and half large plugs. "They're big enough by Mother's Day," says Forrest. "We don't want tall, leggy, soft perennials that may bloom too early or have already bloomed. Ours are tough, hardened-off, more solid plants."

Demand for perennials is also fueled by what people see. "Perennials have become more popular partly because we use them in the landscape designs," he says. Their five designers use perennials throughout the season, and production grows what the designers prefer and can sell. Feedback from the garden centers also affects what Paul and Forrest decide to produce. "If retail asks for it, that's what production grows," says Forrest. "There's good communication between them." Sargent's does buy in some plant material, including potted nursery items and annuals in packs.

Forrest has succeeded in his goal to be "big enough to retain good people and give them responsibility. Nine out of ten times, they do great with it and exceed expectations." Sargent's Landscape Nursery has enjoyed steady growth for over twenty-five years, and Forrest says, "The people that work for us make that happen."

May 1999

Plenty of Dutch Perennials

Debbie Hamrick

How would you like to have all the 'Patriot' hostas in this field? Like other bareroot perennial young plant suppliers in the Netherlands, Jack de Vroomen, Managing Director, De Vroomen Holland, Lisse, the Netherlands, is looking forward to an excellent harvest season after good growing conditions in the summer.

The previous year's digging of peonies and hostas was plagued by heavy rain during the late fall. "We all expected low-quality plants, but the quality was fine," Jack says of the 1998 crop. "The product looked OK, but you never know what is happening internally. Sandy soil and drain pipes saved us."

Since methyl bromide is no longer allowed in the Netherlands, perennial growers won't crop hostas or peonies in the same fields for five years. By rotating crops, pests such as nematodes don't stand a chance.

Like many Dutch bareroot perennial suppliers, De Vroomen produces some of their own plants and buys others in from contract growers. De Vroomen grows out samples of each of the varieties from each contract grower to make sure plants are true to type and to be able to trace back any grow-out problems customers may have. The most popular bareroot perennials: astilbes, hostas, daylilies and peonies.

One of Jack's concerns for the Dutch bareroot perennial market: supply of new varieties. Sometimes companies will widely publicize new varieties, giving them cover spots on catalogs with full knowledge that they don't have enough stock to meet demand, he says. His own rule is that for a new item to be included in the catalog, a minimum of 2,500 must be available, so a wide sampling of customers can try it, Jack says. De Vroomen can be reached at devroomen@flowerbulb.nl.

January 2000

Index

Bold numbers indicate a photograph; italic numbers indicate a table.